Andrea's Story

MELANIE M. LINDHOLM

ANDREA'S STORY

A MEMOIR ABOUT LOVE AND DEATH IN ALASKA

What if the person you loved most was forced to endure inhumane suffering?

At forty-two, Andrea was diagnosed with terminal cancer. With her plan to seek Death With Dignity when she could no longer fight the disease, Andrea fought for nearly three years through 52 rounds of chemo. Trapped in Alaska by COVID-19 in mid-2020, Andrea's plan to legally end her suffering humanely evaporated. Forced to witness her suffering within the U.S. healthcare system's lack of choices for terminal patients, her wife, Melanie, chose love over law in honoring Andrea's wishes.

Andrea's Story is a case study, of sorts, with the goal of championing legislation for both Universal Healthcare and Universal Medical Aid in Dying. By sharing her experience with the world, Melanie hopes to prevent other people from being forced to repeat Andrea's experience. Ultimately, Andrea's Story is a plea for more humane and compassionate options.

DISCLAIMER

This book is a work of non-fiction based on events as understood by the author. However, in order to protect the privacy and safety of individuals involved, certain names, identifying details, locations, and events have been changed, combined, or interpreted differently. The book is not intended to accuse, assign guilt, provide evidence, or make definitive claims. The reader agrees to indemnify and hold the author harmless against any and all claims, suits, charges, orders or judgments brought against the author as a result of any action taken or not taken by the reader.

FORWARD

Andrea wanted her story told. In writing it, I have fulfilled a promise I made to her. This memoir is about her three-year cancer journey, her death, and our experience with the U.S. healthcare system. Prepare yourself for the good, the bad, and the ugly. If you've ever wondered what the nitty-gritty of chemo looks like for terminal cancer patients, this book will give you a good idea. It's also a story about the lack of choices that terminal patients have regarding their own deaths and the struggle that their loved ones endure while trying to honor the wishes of the patient. Set in Interior Alaska, between 2017 and 2020, Andrea's Story is a detailed account of her fearless, fighting spirit and her insights about death, dying, and the decision to die. This memoir is primarily told from my perspective as her caregiver, patient advocate, partner, and soulmate. Full of love and loss, this story is just one of many tragic experiences with cancer, death, and failures of the system in the United States. Ultimately, Andrea's Story is a plea for more humane and compassionate options. By telling her story, I hope to help prevent other people from being forced to repeat her experience.

"To the world, you may be one person. But to one person, you may be the world." – Unknown

CONTENTS

~~

CHAPTER 1: BEFORE THE "C" WORD

The day I met Andrea, my entire world changed. Until that point, I didn't believe in any of the things I was about to experience. I thought "love at first sight" was a myth. But when I saw her walk into my coworker's office, the whole world stopped. It was as if time ceased to exist. I was hyper-focused on the energy coming from her presence. She was a stranger that I was now desperate to know. I watched from my desk as she had a conversation with my coworker. As soon as she left the building, I got up from my desk and went to my coworker's office. When I asked who she was, my coworker said she was a band member and that they'd been discussing an upcoming gig. I asked for her phone number, which my coworker reluctantly gave me, and we immediately began texting each other. Right off the bat, Andrea told me, "I just want you to know that I'm transgender." It was early 2009, and I had never heard that word before, so I didn't know what it meant. Rather than appear stupid, I asked, "What does that mean for you?" She replied, "For me, that means I was born in the wrong body. I was assigned male at birth, but I feel that I'm female in my heart and brain." This was the first time I'd ever heard of such a concept, but I accepted it without question.

From that day forward, I felt undeniably connected to Andrea. The connection was powerful, real, and utterly overwhelming. She felt it as strongly as I did, at the same time I did, as if our energies were in parallel with one another. But we couldn't logically explain it to ourselves, or anyone else. We didn't understand why this would happen, or could happen, given our current life circumstances: We could NOT be together. We were both in committed long-term relationships with our children's other parent. Neither of us was looking for (nor wanting) another partner. This predicament led us to believe that the universe was playing a cruel joke on us. We absolutely needed to be together, but we couldn't be. From the moment we laid eyes on each other, it was as if a rug had been pulled out from under us. Despite what we felt, we couldn't be together because society's rules and norms did not sanction such a breach from the lives we'd already built.

By this point, we'd each spent over 30 years living lives dictated by the expectations of other people. Neither of us had been living authentically. We'd both been raised in conservative Christian religions with harsh lines drawn between right and wrong, acceptance and rejection, sanctioned and unsanctioned. There was little room for deviation. We'd literally been taught, since birth, that conformity was required. The consequence for anything different was risking familial ostracization, social rejection, and even eternal damnation. To allow variety in gender identity, assigned social roles, or religious interpretation was unthinkable.

Nevertheless, here we were, at a crossroad of sorts. We felt deeply connected, as if an otherworldly force was slapping us into another reality, but still feeling an obligation to the lives we'd already built up to that point. For a brief moment, I thought maybe there was a way to straddle both lives, that I could fulfill my obligation to my husband and children while still loving Andrea. In fact, I tried to propose this idea to my husband, but he flatly refused. My attempts to reconcile my two lives, my two loves, my two trajectories, proved to be impossible. After he found out the extent of our connection, my husband demanded that I cut off all communication with Andrea and anyone who had contact with her. He forced me to tearfully delete her number from my phone. He said my obligation was to him and our children, and that any deviation was nothing but fantasy. "You can't live in Disneyland," he said.

Reluctantly, Andrea and I complied with the "no contact" rule. During that time, I became more and more of an empty shell, just going through the motions, on autopilot. My children described me as emotionally unavailable. I felt and acted like a Stepford Wife. I played the part, but lacked the heart and soul required for a convincing performance. I was doing the best I could under the circumstances, but I still felt profound guilt and shame. Like a Stepford Wife, I'd literally been programmed for life as the perfect wife and mother. Operating outside that programming, even briefly, made it impossible for me to unsee or unknow the reality I'd experienced meeting Andrea. I absolutely knew that there was something profoundly significant happening, but I lacked the terminology to adequately explain it. I became more despondent. I was haunted by memories and feelings about Andrea that I couldn't shake. But I kept them all to myself. At one point, I was so depressed and hopeless that I became suicidal. My husband, having completed suicide prevention training required for military personnel, recognized the signs and symptoms. Mentally and emotionally, I was in a very deep, dark place. But I reluctantly answered his questions. Yes, I wanted to die. Yes, I had a plan. Yes, I intended to do it. He said he had "no choice" but to take me to the hospital. Against my will, he made me go. I had no more energy or power left to fight him over this decision. I hated him in that moment; but the truth is, he probably saved my life.

While hospitalized, I was occasionally allowed to use the phone. Having memorized Andrea's phone number, I called her one evening and we talked as if we'd picked up right where we'd left off. Having been hospitalized for suicidality once herself, she very much understood my position and how I was feeling. She assured me, comforted me, and even made me laugh. The nurses in the psych ward overheard me having this conversation on the hallway phone and gave me much more time to talk than the rules allowed, because, they said, "whomever you were talking to seemed to be helping you so much."

However, that was our last conversation. Over the following 3 years, we had no communication. I had no idea what had happened to her. We lived completely separate lives, just like before we'd met, except always feeling a profound connection to each other. That longing for one another was incredibly intense, like a moth drawn to a flame, unable to explain it, but acutely aware that it was life-altering, even potentially life-ending. Without knowing it, we both poured ourselves into our hobbies, our escapes from real life. Mine was dance, hers was music.

By early 2012, my 20-year marriage was failing. The final nail in the coffin, for me, was reading "The Four Love Languages" book, in which I finally realized we were incapable of speaking each other's love language; that despite my best efforts, continued struggle was futile. I felt the creeping feeling of the deep, dark place I'd been in once before, just before my hospitalization. But, this time, I recognized it. I saw it coming. And I knew I would die this time. I knew my choices were either to leave or die. Then suddenly, all of my conscious will and intent disappeared. My body went into "fight or flight" mode. As if by instinct, without consciously thinking, I left. It was an act of self-preservation. I didn't realize what I'd done until I was sitting in a friend's empty house with my belongings. I had no plan, no money, and no hope. I barely held down my minimum wage job, I was incapable of doing things I needed to do for my children, and I had no certainty about anything. My immune system, which had been in survival mode for so long, crashed – hard. I became more physically sick than I'd ever been in my life, before or since. I went to the ER three times because I couldn't breathe due to acute bronchitis. The doctors gave me more prescription drugs than I'd ever taken in my life, before or since.

Three months later, still recovering from illness, I had a random thought about Andrea. I wondered what had happened to her. For all I knew, she might not even be in Alaska anymore. Too afraid to call, I sent her a text message for the first time in 3 years asking how she was doing and if she remembered me. Rather than text back, she immediately called me. "Where are you?" she asked. "I'm at a friend's house, but it's on the opposite side of town," I replied. Then her voice was adamant. "I don't care if you're in China," she said, "I'm coming right now." For the rest of that night, we just held each other and cried, and cried, and cried. We mourned the loss of time, grieving our 3-year separation from each other. We tearfully rejoiced in our energies being reunited, reconnected, reacquainted. We learned that each of us had left our long-term relationships with our children's other parent, that we'd both suffered severely during the 3-years of no contact, and that we both still felt the same intense unexplainable connection to each other. After a lot of talking and counseling, we eventually came to accept that there was only one way to describe our relationship: Soulmates.

For us, being soulmates included unconditional love. We supported each other, worked together, and loved each other without reservation. Andrea supported me through graduate school, and I earned a master's degree. She taught me construction skills, and we literally built a house together. She emotionally supported me through a very painful divorce process. And I was her emotional support during her gender transition. You see, we had made a promise to each other. The deal was: "I'm only going to be with you, if you are you." That meant being true, authentic, genuine, and honest, to ourselves and to each other. I pointed out that she'd lived her whole life to meet other's expectations and that I refused to tolerate that anymore. I advocated and facilitated her becoming true to herself. I helped her file for legal name change, start hormone therapy, and change gender markers on government documents. This was an exciting, scary, new journey. But we did it together, now as fiancées.

However, the rest of the world didn't have the same commitment to love, acceptance, and understanding. As if grad school, divorce, house construction, and gender transition wasn't enough, we also had to deal with the blatant discrimination that led to Andrea losing her job. Many transgender people experience loss of employment, housing, and relationships with family and friends as a result of becoming true to who they really are. Andrea was no exception. Somebody at work refused to accept her name and pronouns, then made it their mission to get her fired. That's a whole story in and of itself. Long story short, through no fault of her own, Andrea became unemployed, and we lost the income we needed to finish building our house. It was devastating. But not as devastating as what was about to come. Little did we know Andrea already had cancer. In fact, she might have developed cancer as a direct result of working that job.

To add insult to injury, this was during the first Trump administration. In political and legal arenas, people debated the existence of, humanity of, and rights of transgender or gender-non-conforming people. It was unclear whether Andrea had equal rights to military service, employment, housing, or medical care. Policies and laws changed almost daily, both nationally and locally. I testified on her behalf several times when legislation was open for public testimony. I spoke about the discrimination she had experienced and why she deserved the same rights as me. This wasn't just about which bathroom she was allowed to pee in. This was life or death. Overall, transgender people have higher rates of suicide and homicide. For transwomen, it's even higher, especially for non-whites. Andrea was half Native American (Pottawatomie Tribe). Many Indigenous cultures held great honor and respect for transgender and gender-non-conforming people, but colonial capitalist white Christian America certainly did not. I was keenly aware of this as a result of my graduate thesis research, but my primary motivation to advocate for Andrea came from love.

In 2016, Andrea had been diagnosed with a blood disorder called Polycythemia Vera, which meant her body was making too many red blood cells. When her doctor explained that she was now at significant increased risk for stroke and heart attack, she was forced to eliminate any other risk factors. For Andrea, that meant two things: 1) stop hormone therapy, and 2) stop smoking cigarettes. Amazingly, she stopped both instantly, almost overnight. While I was extremely happy that she quit smoking, I was devastated that she was now medically unable to continue her physical gender transition. I was distraught over what I perceived to be an injustice. After we had many discussions, I admitted that I wanted her to "pass" as a cisgender woman in order to avoid discrimination in the real world that didn't love her the way I did. But, Andrea assured me, this was of little concern to her. Essentially, she said, "I am who I am. Take it or leave it. I don't need anyone's permission or validation. If they can't accept me for who I am, regardless of whether I 'pass' or not, then they don't deserve to be part of my life." One time, I witnessed Andrea repeating that same message to her mother during a phone conversation. I thought for sure that would be the end of their relationship; but thankfully, I was wrong.

Despite wearing nothing but jeans and T-shirts, Andrea unapologetically used her female name and pronouns, as did I. At times, I militantly corrected other people. If anyone used her former name or pronouns, I felt a rage inside me. I couldn't stop myself from constantly defending her. She'd see how worked up I'd get, especially at family get-togethers, when the wrong name or pronoun slipped out. In private, she told me that she'd "given up" on her family really accepting her and using the right name and pronouns. She asked me to stop trying to correct them, but I absolutely refused. And I only became more adamant in defending her after her cancer diagnosis. I felt strongly, and still do, that after all the indignity and injustice she'd already experienced in her life, she certainly didn't deserve to experience more of that in her death.

By summer 2017, Andrea was having several symptoms of colon cancer, although we didn't know it yet. I remember her telling me about her physical symptoms, and I responded with, "That doesn't seem right. Something is wrong. We should go to the doctor." We kept going to the doctor, over and over, for months. But all of them assumed that there couldn't be anything serious because Andrea was relatively young and otherwise healthy. She was given special enemas, medications, sleep studies, suggestions for positive thinking and the like, for months, doing nothing to alleviate her symptoms. Finally, in November 2017, the flabbergasted internal medicine doctor said, "I cannot explain why you continue to have symptoms, so let's do a test to rule out anything crazy." He put in a referral for Andrea to get a colonoscopy despite the fact that she was too young for a screening. The prep was extremely painful for her, which only proved to bolster my suspicions that something was seriously wrong. But it wasn't until the doctor completed the colonoscopy procedure, with Andrea still unconscious, that I first heard the "C" word. He walked up close to me, made eye contact, and with a concernedly soft voice, said, "I won't know for sure until the pathology report comes back from the lab, but I'm pretty damn sure that what I saw in there was cancer."

Shocked and unsure, Andrea and I resolved to withhold our judgment on the matter until we received the pathology report and the CT scan results that followed. However, that limbo-land was short lived, as both results soon confirmed our worst fears. The only person unconvinced by the reports was Dr. Conley, the surgeon who was assigned to our case. Dr. Conley basically ignored the radiology report and said we couldn't really know unless we looked inside during surgery. We were told that the goal of surgery was a colon resection, in which the part of the colon with cancer is removed and the healthy ends sewn back together. However, if, for some reason that procedure wasn't possible, then a port would be surgically placed in Andrea's chest for chemotherapy purposes. In other words, Dr. Conley explained, if the colon resection failed, then chemo was the only other available treatment option.

Andrea's surgery was scheduled for mid-December 2017, just as I was trying to finish teaching fall semester at the university, with another contract already signed to teach Wintermester during early January 2018. And, ironically, I already had my own surgery scheduled for mid-January to get a necessary hysterectomy to prevent inevitable cervical cancer. The reality that we'd both be recovering from major surgery at the same time was terrifying. Reluctantly, I was forced to reach out for help and support, which is very difficult for me to do. I'm a giver. I'm happy to give to others, but I won't let others give to me (unless under extreme duress). If nothing else, this was a lesson in humility for me and became the testing grounds for who would become our support network. Thankfully, family and friends willingly stepped up with all kinds of support: meals, errands, cleaning, bills, listening and understanding. My recovery was 6 weeks, but Andrea's was much longer. Her severely compromised body took over 3 months to heal from surgery enough to be able to start chemotherapy.

However, what I remember most, and what had the biggest emotional impact on all of us, was the report from Dr. Conley just after emerging from Andrea's surgery. Even after I heard Dr. Conley explain it to me, then again to Andrea's family and friends who were waiting with me, I still couldn't wrap my brain around what had happened in the operating room. As I understand it, when the surgeon got inside Andrea's abdomen, it was filled with tumors. They were literally everywhere. Her entire abdominal cavity was completely covered in thousands of little tumors. The photos taken from inside reminded me of constellations of stars in the night sky. The surgeon quickly realized there was no possible way to do a colon resection. It was impossible to surgically remove the tumors since they had clearly grown far outside the colon. Dr. Conley had no choice except to take tissue samples, install the chemo port in Andrea's chest, and send us home. All conclusions confirmed the worst-case scenario: Stage IV Cancer. Nobody ever used the term "terminal cancer" with us; but later, we figured it out.

While in the recovery room, still drowsy from the anesthesia, the first thing Andrea said to her daughter: "Well, kiddo, at least you got a dad for 25 years." Andrea's daughter and I were in tears, but Andrea was calm and matter of fact. She had feared for a long time that she would be given some kind of catastrophic diagnosis and had described herself as a hypochondriac, even before I met her. It's almost as if her body and mind knew something was coming and was trying to prepare her or warn her. However, I was in denial, and stayed in denial for years, because I simply wasn't willing to believe that the universe would get us together just to tear us apart. And I also believed there must exist a magic formula or combination of protocols that could cure her cancer. At times, I obsessed over special diets and supplements, regimens that other cancer patients had success with, and all kinds of recommendations I'd found on the Internet.

Andrea definitely did her fair share of this, too, and ended up landing on RSO, Rick Simpson Oil, named for the man who invented the method for extraction. RSO is similar to FECO (full extract cannabis oil); both available online, but too expensive for us to afford. However, Andrea discovered that Rick Simpson's method was open source, meaning that the details of his extraction process were published online for free. So, Andrea set out to engineer her own cost-effective, homemade version using easily accessible components. Over a few months, by trial and error, Andrea perfected her own distillation process so that the extraction method would be sustainable for us. Fortunately, Alaska was already a legal state and she'd already been growing her own cannabis prior to her diagnosis. But now, she needed to ramp up production in order to produce enough plant material for the recommended RSO levels required for treatment of Stage IV cancer. She later taught me how to grow, harvest, and process the plants using the equipment she'd modified, all the way to putting oil in capsules for her to swallow. We did much of this process together; but near the end, I was doing it by myself since she didn't have the strength.

The day she came home from surgery, Andrea stayed up all night talking with her best friend, Gabby. In that conversation, Andrea said she didn't want to suffer. In fact, she had already thought of ways to end her suffering, some involving guns, others involving ways to "disappear." Andrea wanted to end her life herself in the event her diagnosis caused intolerable suffering. She also voiced a strong desire to spare her loved ones the pain of watching her suffer. In Alaska, as in most states, there is no legal avenue to end suffering for the terminally ill. We later learned that there had been 2 proposals to offer a legal option in the state of Alaska, sponsored by Representative Harriet Drummond: HB 99 during the 2015-2016 session called VOLUNTARY TERMINATION OF LIFE, followed by HB 54 during the 2017-2018 session called TERMINALLY ILL: ENDING LIFE OPTION. Neither passed. The fact that the legislation failed ended up directly impacting Andrea. If either bill had passed, Andrea would have had a legal choice available by the time she needed it.

We quickly realized we were in over our heads. Not only were there no legal ways out of suffering, but there was a steep learning curve to navigating suffering. After a serious diagnosis, patients and their families often fumble around, attempting to learn how the healthcare system works, fighting their insurance companies, dealing with the everyday realities of living with their illnesses, and struggling to maintain desperately needed relationships with others. I felt obligated to learn how to do all this so that I could be Andrea's advocate. I was also feeling bombarded by many well-meaning friends and family who sent emails, texts, and Facebook messages requesting updates on Andrea's condition, offering recommendations, and asking what they could do to help. I simply didn't have the capacity to adequately respond to everyone; it was more than I could keep up with. Thankfully, my coworker suggested creating a private Facebook group that only included Andrea's close friends and family so that there was a central location for everyone to get updates and offer support. I proposed this idea to Andrea, and she gave me permission to create the group. Each time I wanted to post an update, I got Andrea's approval before posting. She also had administrative rights to the page, as did her daughter. Showing her sense of humor, Andrea named her group page "Andrea's Shitty Ass Cancer."

While recovering from surgery, Andrea decided she didn't completely believe or agree with her diagnosis. So, she requested a second opinion. Several people recommended Dr. Gold, an expert in colon cancer at Swedish Cancer Institute in Seattle, who had been practicing oncology for 30 years. However, her insurance, Alaska State Medicaid, told us that they generally did not cover the cost of second opinions. At this point, Andrea had been unemployed for 26 months, which is why she qualified for Medicaid. We were grateful for Medicaid because there's no way that my income could've paid for her colonoscopy, CT scans, and surgery. But getting Alaska Medicaid to pay for her second opinion proved to be challenging. We got the run-around. Seattle said they needed a referral from Fairbanks. But Fairbanks said they didn't do referrals. But a referral is also required for insurance to cover the second opinion. Of course, Fairbanks doesn't want to lose patients. It's not in their best interest to do a referral elsewhere because that means they lose business. There's no motivation for them to do it. After a lot of persistence on my part, I finally persuaded the surgeon to send the referral and the oncologist to send Andrea's medical records to Seattle. Alaska Medicaid made an exception in Andrea's case because of her Stage IV diagnosis, but only to cover the appointment with Dr. Gold for the second opinion. We had one week to figure out how to arrange travel and lodging on our own. Fortunately, Andrea's friend Rhees used his airline miles to get our tickets, and her friend Sarah who lives in Seattle offered us ground transportation and lodging. We were so grateful for amazing friends for making that important trip possible. Unfortunately, Andrea's symptoms worsened. She had a high pain tolerance, but it was getting to be unbearable. She feared the hardest part would be surviving the plane ride while being in pain and having to use the bathroom a lot.

While we waited for our trip to Seattle, the Fairbanks oncologist was still reluctant to give any definitive prognosis or timescale. After we pressured him, the doctor finally admitted, "I can't predict lifespan or effectiveness of treatment because everyone is different. But the average lifespan of someone with Stage IV colon cancer – if doing chemo – is about 5 years." Most disappointing, the only treatment he offered was chemo. He said there were no other options for us to consider. Afterword, Andrea said, "It's pretty obvious that the pharmaceutical industry has the doctors in their pocket. If it's not making money for the industry, then they're not interested in looking at alternative treatments for their patients."

Andrea only attempted to do chemotherapy once before going to Seattle, but she had a severe anxiety attack. It was one of the worst I'd ever witnessed. Her port and incision sites had been extremely painful since surgery. After attempting to access her port for a routine blood draw, the pain triggered an anxiety attack. She said she wanted the port removed and refused the chemo treatment. The doctor prescribed Lidocaine patches to put on her port site, but the insurance denied it. Andrea said, "You know, because insurance companies get to decide what patients need, not their doctors!" (Ironically, I'd gone through that myself the month before. I tried dealing directly with my insurance company denying something I'd already been approved for. I had to write a letter pleading my case and why I needed the treatment recommended by my doctor to appeal their decision. But I was still denied. So, I had to pay hundreds of dollars out-of-pocket). Fortunately for Andrea, a friend gave her some Lidocaine patches and that was her saving grace for keeping the port pain under control. Later, we found out the stitches used to keep the port in place had "tails" that hadn't been cut, so they were stabbing her from underneath, and eventually came through her skin. They never granted her wish to remove the port; she died with it still in her chest.

In addition to anxiety, pain, loss of appetite, drastic weight loss and constant nausea, there was legitimate concern for a bowel obstruction. The doctor tried to get the insurance to approve an MRI, but at the last minute the radiologist decided a CT scan was a better way to see what they wanted to see. The suspected blockage was a significant narrowing, but still cause for concern because a narrowing can become a blockage. When I picked up the radiology report from the cancer center, the nurse handed it to me and said, "Go to Swedish." The tone of her voice said: this is serious. The report also had other concerns: a lesion on her liver that had grown since the last CT along with greater metastasis and thickening of colon, peritoneum, and omentum. That explained why Andrea's symptoms had worsened.

Despite her suffering, Andrea survived the trip to Seattle. The oncologist, Dr. Gold, surprised us by saying he had patients who had been doing chemotherapy for ten consecutive years. We had no idea people did chemo that long. It was daunting to think we could be doing it long-term. He recommended Andrea do chemo, but supplement it with supportive care, such as "partnering" of Eastern and Western medicine. Andrea would have more options for holistic care and "partnering" with other clinics (such as naturopathic, acupuncture, Palliative Care, etc.) in Seattle. But we had to weigh those benefits against the disadvantages of traveling (which can be miserable when you already don't feel well). We packed in as much as possible into 1.5 days: we saw the oncologist, the education center, the Palliative Care doctor, and a total of 3 amazing social workers who were able to validate and support us. Andrea and I felt we were finally listened to regarding our long list of concerns. Besides getting a second opinion, it was worth going to Swedish Cancer Institute to be heard (we certainly didn't experience that level of care/competence in Fairbanks). The Palliative Care doctor prescribed Scopolamine for Andrea's constant nausea, which we wish she'd been offered sooner (another example of the substandard care in Fairbanks). But when I went to pick up the anti-nausea Scopolamine prescription at the pharmacy, they said insurance wouldn't cover it. Out-of-pocket cost was $27 PER PATCH (one patch lasts 72 hours). To add insult to injury, Dr. Gold said Andrea's painful incision sites were now cancerous. He said it was very unfortunate that Andrea had a general surgeon in Fairbanks. He said she should have had a colorectal surgeon or a cancer surgeon (another example of the limited options in Fairbanks). And he said Andrea's $30,000 surgery may not have even been necessary. He said we shouldn't have trusted Dr. Conley (the general surgeon) to interpret the radiology report. Instead, we should've asked for a copy of the CT images before agreeing to surgery. They clearly showed the cancer had metastasized and was not operable. Andrea worked in the radiology field for 13 years and she knew better, but the surgeon was so adamant about doing surgery, and Andrea was too sick to argue. Now, 3 months later, those incisions had opened the door for cancer to grow inside them.

Thankfully, everyone we encountered at Swedish Cancer Institute (and Seattle in general) were very progressive and accepting regarding transgender people. They rarely got pronouns wrong, and when they did, they corrected themselves immediately. Upon returning to Fairbanks, Andrea had the difficult task of weighing all her options, assessing the advantages and disadvantages, and deciding what she wanted to do. She'd have more comprehensive care in Seattle, but the traveling and logistics proved too challenging. Ultimately, she decided to stay in Fairbanks, mostly because we couldn't afford to cover the costs of moving or traveling to Seattle.

By this point, I'd been forced to change jobs. I could no longer work 2-3 jobs outside the home. I needed to be able to be home in my role as caregiver to my fiancée and accompany her for treatments. Fortunately, I signed a contract for my dream job using my graduate degree and research interests that allowed me to work from home or wherever I could take my laptop. This allowed me to work in my field and still be Andrea's caretaker and patient advocate. I was "all in" to fight this battle with her. But Andrea had reservations. She felt guilty for becoming ill and for putting me in the position of caregiver. But most of all, she didn't want me to see her suffer. She made several attempts to convince me to abandon her. She said, "Melanie, you need to leave. Go to Canada now. You don't deserve to watch me suffer. You shouldn't have to watch me die." Every time she repeated this, I'd argue with her about how love doesn't work that way; I couldn't just leave her. Finally, after several failed attempts, I came up with a response that worked. I asked her: "If the roles were reversed, what would you do?" After a long silence, she replied, "I would stay and take care of you no matter what." "Yes," I said, "then let me do the same for you."

CHAPTER 2: ANOTHER "C" WORD

My favorite memories with Andrea involve building our house together. We were both so full of hopes and dreams for our future. It was very hard work, but we loved working together. She was so patient with me, teaching me all her construction skills along the way. At the beginning, I was terrified of heights and power tools. By the end, I was roofing alone and cutting lumber more accurately than her. We poured our hearts, souls, blood, sweat, tears, time, and money into that house. Andrea said this was her dream house, that she intended to live in it for the rest of her life, so she insisted on building everything she'd ever wanted. I complained about the large size being difficult to heat during Alaska's winters, that we didn't need 17-foot vaulted ceilings. But Andrea was adamant about what she wanted, saying this was the one and only time she would ever do this, and that she intended to grow old in this house. She also said she would've never built it without me, that nobody else would've ever done this with her. Indeed, we made a great team. We even started helping our friends with their remodeling and construction projects. Andrea seemed so full of life and purpose – even though she was most likely Stage II or III during that time. Little did I know, I would soon watch that vibrant life become impaired and hindered by yet another "C" word: chemo.

After her diagnosis, Andrea refused to reconsider starting chemo until both she and I had fully recovered from our surgeries. In her case, she especially needed to gain weight before doing chemo (she'd lost 20 pounds since her surgery); she had no appetite – a common problem for cancer patients. Eventually, since there were no other treatment options given to her, Andrea began chemotherapy at the Fairbanks Memorial Hospital's Cancer Center in early April 2018. I remember the physician's assistant asking, "Has anyone explained your diagnosis to you?" Andrea replied, "Yes," because, after all, we had heard the "C" word (cancer). However, nobody ever said the word "terminal." So, in hindsight, no, we never really had her diagnosis explained to us. Every single medical professional we interacted with during Andrea's 3-year battle avoided saying the word "terminal" at all costs. Like the elephant in the room, nobody in the healthcare world wanted to acknowledge the reality of our situation. It seemed that only people outside that world used the word "terminal." The very first time we heard that word was about six months after Andrea's diagnosis when we went to see a grief counselor named Sally. Sally explained how she'd worked in hospice for 20 years and about how her own mother had died of cancer. She was the first and only person who was straightforward with us about the inevitability of Andrea's death – but we didn't want to hear it. In fact, Andrea refused to return for any more counseling sessions with Sally. But I continued to go by myself – simply because I needed someone to talk to about everything without further burdening our friends. And, truth be told, we still held out hope that Andrea could somehow beat the odds.

Anyone who has ever done chemotherapy can tell you that the side effects are absolutely awful. Sometimes, when I posted updates on Andrea's cancer Facebook page, I'd start with a disclaimer: "If you don't want to know the gory details, stop reading now." During Andrea's first chemo treatment, without anyone saying it, we slowly began to realize that it was essentially an all-day affair of pumping poison into her port. Toward the end of the day, they gave her a powerful anti-nausea drug that had to be activated by a steroid before they could give her the final chemo drug. We warned them that she had SEVERE reactions to steroids. They noted our concern, but said they still had to give the drugs anyway. I watched as Andrea grew more and more irritable. By the time we got home, she was in full "roid rage." She broke things, yelled at people and pets, rage cried, said she was having homicidal and suicidal thoughts, and sprained her finger by slamming it on the table while yelling, "Why the hell am I so damn angry?!" Andrea's mother cleaned up broken glass, waited for me to come back from the pharmacy with Andrea's other medications, then took the dog and the guns for safekeeping.

The steroid reaction wasn't the only drug complication. Immediately, even before we left the hospital, Andrea started experiencing neuropathy and EXTREME sensitivity to cold – a common side effect of one of the chemo drugs. Just walking a few steps to the car was excruciating for her. Taking something out of the refrigerator caused her extreme pain. Anything below body temperature felt like a thousand needles in her fingertips when she touched it. The same reaction happened to her mouth and throat if she tried to eat/drink something. So, she started wearing gloves all the time and I started warming all her food/drinks to body temp or higher. She rarely left the house, as Alaska weather is almost always below body temperature.

The all-day affair of pumping poison into her port didn't end when we left the hospital. They hooked her up with a portable infusion pump that she had to wear for 3 days, commonly called a "juice box," that administered chemo drugs after she went home.

There was an IV line that ran from the pump to her port. That line was a hazard; it hurt when the line got pulled or accidentally caught on something. So, there she was, running to get in the front door because the cold was so painful, only to be jumped on by the dog (who was always excited when we got home) nearly pulling out the pump line – which was the other reason the dog got yelled at and sent to Grandma's house.

After I picked up all her drugs from the pharmacy, I noticed one of them was a steroid. Despite Andrea's extreme reaction to the first one, they'd prescribed more! She asked me to call first thing the next morning to tell them, "There's no way in hell she's taking the steroid." They said if Andrea could manage her nausea with the other prescriptions, plus cannabis oil, then she didn't have to take the steroid. They also reminded us to keep in mind that, because of the chemo, all of Andrea's body secretions would be toxic. She had to use a separate bathroom to avoid exposing others. Unless I wore gloves, I was not allowed to clean up vomit, diarrhea, or urine. If we had intercourse, we had to use condoms.

There was a long list of other awful side effects from the chemo drugs, including a nasty rash that covered her entire body, painful mouth sores, irregular heartbeat, blood in her urine/stool, extreme fatigue, swelling, vomiting, diarrhea, constant nausea, and weight loss. Those were the common ones. Then there was a long list of rare and serious side effects as well. And, to think, the very first oncologist we'd met with told us that nausea was the only side effect! Talk about not being honest with your patients!

Right off the bat, I was exhausted trying to stay on top of all the different medications, when to administer them, trying to get her to eat and drink properly, keeping the pets off her, cleaning, cooking, managing insurance/doctors/appointments, transporting, shopping, working my jobs, and trying to take care of my-self so that I didn't burn out. Being a chemo patient was awful, for sure; but being a caregiver was also taxing. Nobody wants to see the person they love suffering. And, as hard as caregivers try, they can't magically fix everything. Despite my best efforts, Andrea continued to experience pain, loss of normal functions, drug side effects, depression, anxiety, and suffering. All of that, with no guarantee of survival.

As grueling as 3 days of poison pumping was, we soon learned that she really went downhill when they removed her pump. She was so sick and weak that she couldn't eat or take her medications. The worst side effects seemed to hit days later. I remember thinking, "Cancer sucks. Chemo sucks. Fighting insurance companies sucks. I hope that someday in the future, we will look back and think it was barbaric to do things this way." In her limited capacity, Andrea made brief Facebook posts as a computer programmer:

```
<up_date>
Chemo sux!
</up_date>
```

It was a rough "chemo initiation" for us. They say the first round is a bit of trial and error because everyone reacts differently. In Andrea's case, the absolute worst day was the first day after the pump was removed. She said she felt like she was dying. She couldn't get out of bed, couldn't eat, and felt absolutely miserable. She was down to 138 pounds, which I believed to be completely unacceptable. She couldn't eat for 3 days. I called the Cancer Center nurses repeatedly until they finally told us to come in. Andrea barely hobbled in there, looking like death. But then, MAGIC happened. They gave her an IV with saline and anti-nausea meds that brought her back to life. By the time we left, she was joking with nurses and asking me if we could stop by the music store on the way home. I was shocked. It was a night and day difference. By that evening, she was able to eat and do band practice – a complete turn-around from the previous day.

Two weeks from her first round, Andrea's second round of chemo fell on her birthday, April 16th. She turned 43 and I made her a birthday cake out of fruit that I assembled in the back of her car in the Cancer Center parking lot. She and I ate it during the all-day affair of pumping poison into her port. This was around the time that I had started to put the pieces together regarding this chemo business. In Andrea's case, it was not a cure. Rather, it was supposed to extend her expected life span and reduce her cancer symptoms. But considering the side effects, pain, and suffering induced by chemo, it seemed to me that she was essentially trading quality for quantity. Extension of life meant extension of suffering. Considering the medical oath of "do no harm," then it seemed unethical to put somebody through so much pain/suffering with no guarantee that it would work. With chemo, there was no assurance that it would even be worth it. Of course, everyone is different. For some, it works. For others, it doesn't. So, people take the chance and then hope the suffering pays off. Andrea was one of those people. She chose the suffering. I didn't always agree with her choices, but I always supported her – no matter what.

As if excessive weight loss, fatigue and nausea wasn't miserable enough, the second round gave Andrea several more chemo side effects preventing her from eating: painful, bleeding, cracking external and internal mouth sores, and extremely painful salivary glands (think of the reaction you had if you've ever tried a sour Warhead, only 100 times worse). It was already a challenge to make all food/drinks at body temperature (due to extreme cold sensitivity) and stay on top of the nausea, but the painful mouth issues made eating nearly impossible. We had the prescription for "magic mouthwash" that helped momentarily with eating, but it was very expensive. She refused to take painkillers because they all had side effects (nausea, abdominal pain, constipation) that she had enough of already. Also, her immune system really took a hit (her white blood cell count dropped dangerously low). Combined, all this threatened her ability to do the third round.

As miserable as this was, there were sweet silver linings. When Andrea was feeling super sick, our kitty cat Tigerlilly would come to snuggle and lend a paw to help Andrea feel better. When Andrea managed to make it to her third round, our Facebook update read, "Good news: we started another round of chemo. Bad news: we started another round of chemo. Cancer is a bitch. You're either so sick you need to do chemo, or you're so sick because you did chemo. Either way sucks."

We experimented with a couple new things in the third round that helped. Andrea asked for IV fluids on the day they pulled the pump out to help prevent the crash that had happened every time and that strategy worked. She still had plenty of chemo side effects (skin rash, fatigue, nausea, weight loss, cold sensitivity) but she didn't completely crash for days like the other times. It was the first time I didn't have to take her back to get IV fluids in the days following the pump being pulled, so that was an improvement. But we ended up going back twice again anyway because she had to get injections of Granix (Filgrastim) to help stimulate her bone marrow to increase white blood cell count (her WBC counts were progressively dropping, and the doctor didn't want that trend to continue any further). When we got a follow-up blood draw, the WBC count had come back up, so the injections worked. Those small steps gave her just enough hope to keep going.

Then we got the first bill. Andrea's first month of treatment was over $40,000. We had no idea how much one month of chemotherapy cost in Alaska, but we soon found out that standard treatment for Andrea's Stage IV colon cancer easily cost between $40,000 and $45,000 per month. Just one of her chemo drugs, Cetuximab, cost $15,480 for each 10mg dose. When I mentioned our shock upon learning this, the oncologist said he had patients who received injections that cost $25,000 each, and the patient had to get one every 2 weeks. So that was $50,000 per month, for one patient, for just one drug! I wondered how in the world this could be sustainable at a national level. I started to realize that even patients with "good" insurance were still paying 20% of those costs, which Andrea and I would never afford (which is why Medicaid had to step in). I tried to imagine how many Americans could afford that 20% (about $8,000 per month) if they were given Andrea's diagnosis in Alaska. I began to question whether it was ethical for a for-profit system to benefit from people's suffering. After all, they know people will literally pay ANYTHING when their life is on the line. Patients are easy to exploit for profits when they're desperate.

I soon decided there would never be a cure for cancer – not when chemotherapy costs $40,000 to $50,000 per month, per patient. It's so lucrative! Big Pharma was making too much money on that gig. And they had the power to suppress or sabotage anything else that threatened their continued profits. The cost of one month of Andrea's chemo was double what I made in a year. One of the nurses at the Cancer Center referred to the system as "criminal." Andrea's mother called it "medical extortion." There's a reason 'Breaking Bad' was such a popular American TV show (the main character starts making meth to pay for his cancer treatments) because people felt nearly forced into illegal activity in order to afford healthcare.

In early May 2018, Andrea's ANC was 846, which meant her immune system was too weak to handle more chemo. This was the first of many times we were told she would have to wait a week to try again. I was glad that she would have a week to try to gain some much-needed weight. A week later, Andrea successfully completed round 4. Again, they wanted us to come back for Granix injections the following two days to keep her white blood cell counts from dropping. A follow-up CT scan was ordered and scheduled for June 1st so we could see if chemo was working or not. By this time, Andrea had developed yet another side effect. Her hands were cracked, painful, and burning. Thanks to special lotion, she was able to get a little bit of relief. But skin is the largest organ of the body, so it made sense that chemo and immune deficiency would show signs there. The good news was that Andrea's first follow-up CT scan results showed the cancer had slightly decreased mass and there was no new cancer; that was the best result we could have hoped for after 4 cycles of chemo. The bad news was that didn't change her treatment plan; we still had to continue with the very aggressive chemo drugs on the every-two-week-regimen (which felt grueling). I remember asking the oncologist about how many rounds of chemo they expected Andrea to do. He replied that he wanted Andrea to do at least 12 rounds. At the time, that seemed almost impossible to me. But, in true fighter fashion, Andrea blew everyone's expectations out of the water by completing a total of 52 rounds before entering hospice care.

Round 5 in mid-May proved to be an especially hard "chemo crash," as we called it. Since she couldn't get out of bed, Andrea decided to call the Social Security Administration to inquire about her disability application (that our friend insisted we file back in

December shortly following Andrea's surgery). After 4 hours on hold, Andrea finally spoke with a representative who flatly explained that the Social Security Administration had 6 months to accept or reject the application. In her sick, chemo crashed voice, Andrea said, "I don't know if I'll still be alive by then." The representative was taken aback, silent for a moment, then said he'd see what he could do. Magically, a week later, her application was approved. Those who have ever applied for disability know this is almost unheard of. Usually, the first application is denied as a matter of practice. Patients and their families often spend years applying and re-applying, submitting exorbitant medical records, and only get approved after hiring an attorney, if at all. At the time, I believed Andrea's application had been approved as a result of that phone call. But some of our knowledgeable friends said it was due to her diagnosis, which led me to consider that her condition was much worse than I believed it to be. I was still holding out hope that she could somehow beat cancer, that all this wretched chemo would be worth it, that her fierce warrior spirit would win; I simply wasn't willing to accept that the universe would get us together just to tear us apart. Either way, the benefits from SSDI (that Andrea had paid into her entire working life) was a godsend for us; it enabled us to pay basic living expenses like heat, water, food, and electricity.

In early June, Andrea reported to a chemo nurse that she was experiencing symptoms of what was called "visual artifact." This was cause for concern, as chemo drugs can affect the brain and vision of some patients. The Cancer Center immediately ordered an MRI and the results showed Andrea had an aneurysm on the anterior communicating artery in her brain. Because brain aneurysms can be lethal, they recommend reducing anything that would put pressure on her circulatory system. In other words, no strenuous activity, stress, or anything that could elevate her BP. The doctor then ordered an MRA so they could see the entire brain arterial map in better detail. However, we had to wait for Medicaid to approve the order. Technically, Medicaid had 20 days to approve or reject the doctor's order. But because Andrea's case was urgent, the doctor tried to push Medicaid approval through in just 3 days. In the meantime, we were told that if there were any changes in Andrea's symptoms, we had to go to the ER immediately. Depending on the results of the MRA, she would then be given a referral to a neurosurgeon for treatment options – possibly brain surgery.

As you might imagine, the news of Andrea's brain aneurysm was difficult news for us to cope with. As if cancer and chemo wasn't enough already! We both spent that morning crying and talking. Eventually, we had to force ourselves to stop because tears burned the skin of Andrea's chemo-cracked cheeks. The social worker at the Cancer Center had been encouraging us for months to seek therapy/counseling to get professional help dealing with everything we were going through. But again, Medicaid was a barrier to those services. There was only one counseling option in Fairbanks that accepted Medicaid, and they had long wait lists and stringent criteria to be accepted. With a second life-threatening medical diagnosis, Andrea said I didn't deserve to go through all this because of her, that it wasn't fair to me, that I should go have a happy life without her keeping me down, that she would break up with me so that I could be free to live in Canada and pursue my dreams, even if she had to commit suicide to make that happen. Perhaps we needed to talk to a qualified person about all that? Medicaid didn't think so. And they took their time approving the MRA until Andrea said, "I'm going on a hunger strike." She put up enough of a fuss that they finally managed to get Medicaid approval and her MRA was scheduled for the following day. Everything magically worked as soon as they found out she was suicidal.

At this point, I reluctantly accepted the reality that I needed to give up teaching at the university. This meant a loss of income and I feared being unable to make the payments on my credit cards that I'd maxed out building the house (which was still unfinished). I was struggling with how to continue earning money while caring for Andrea. Nearly every aspect of our lives had been affected by cancer and our whole lives now revolved around her chemo cycle. I remember wishing that someone at the Cancer Center had sat us down and explained how our lives would be turned upside down, how we would need to adjust to all the changes, and what resources existed to help us do that. Later, we learned that the Cancer Center had a person who was supposed to do those kinds of things, called a Nurse Navigator, but we had fallen through the cracks during staff turnover. So, I was on my own to navigate how in the world I could continue meeting my financial responsibilities while working as a full-time caregiver. When asked how things were going, I expressed this struggle to an acquaintance at a potluck. Another potluck attendee overheard me talking, and said, "Melanie, you're already doing the job. You might as well get paid for it. You need to apply at Access Alaska." I had no idea what she was talking about; I'd never heard of Access Alaska before. I left the potluck, went home, and did some online research about Access Alaska. I discovered they had programs for people with virtually any disability, matching needed services with caregivers who could provide them. And the only reason I would be allowed to provide caregiving services for Andrea was because we weren't legally married yet (spouses cannot be caregivers to their disabled spouse under these government programs, and their income affects their disability benefits, meaning that most disabled Americans live in perpetual poverty). Most of those programs are funded by Medicare and Medicaid, so the processing and paperwork was lengthy. I applied to be Andrea's caregiver in June, completed the required training, waited for Medicaid approval, and finally got my first paycheck in December. That meant I'd been caring for Andrea for a whole year before I started getting paid for doing that job. And it wasn't much money either. Between my computer job, Andrea's disability benefits and Access Alaska, it was just enough to keep us afloat. But it wasn't enough to cover anything beyond basic living expenses. So, I wrote letters to all my credit card companies explaining my situation and offered them plans to pay what I could.

Discover was the only credit card company who refused my payment plan. They sued me in court, and they won. By so doing, they forced me into bankruptcy. Since I couldn't afford an attorney, I had to represent myself. I attended a one-day workshop to learn how to complete the mountain of paperwork required, then worked for months filling it out and gathering all the supporting documents. I spent a lot of time and tears in the process. I had to learn to become a bankruptcy attorney at the same time I was taking care of a terminal cancer patient, house, pets, and working my computer job. When I got overwhelmed and frustrated, I would remind myself that I had earned a master's degree. Surely, I had the skills to learn how to file and represent myself in bankruptcy court. But it was the injustice of being put in that position due to my partner's cancer diagnosis that didn't sit well with me. I wasn't the patient, but I was forced into bankruptcy anyway. I wondered how many other families had been in similar predicaments due to a loved one's illness. Finally, after six months of paperwork and processing, my bankruptcy was final. This meant I was released from the credit card debt, but nothing else. And it meant I was banned from receiving any kind of credit for the next 7 years. Thankfully, the State of Alaska allowed us to keep our house – only because it was unfinished and therefore too difficult to sell.

Andrea continued doing rounds of chemo every two weeks, followed by CT scans every 6-8 weeks to track changes. Ironically, both chemo and CT scans cause cancer. Chemo drugs and doses of radiation take a toll on the body. Andrea had worked 13 years in a hospital – much of that time in radiology – so she was aware of the risks. In fact, her father believed that all those years working in that environment had exposed her to radiation (either intentionally or accidentally) and was the reason she got cancer. The hospital stopped requiring employees to wear radiation detection devices soon after she started working there, and it was well known that the coworker who ultimately caused her to lose her job wanted to harm her any way he could, so it's possible Andrea could've been exposed. However, Andrea believed she was more susceptible to cancer due to a combination of high stress, poor diet, drinking, and smoking cigarettes. Whatever the cause(s), we would never really know. All that mattered to us now was how to survive. Andrea's oncologist periodically decided to delay her treatment, most often due to her blood draw results showing signs of a weak immune system. Cancer weakens the immune system and chemo kills off the white blood cells, so the doctor had legitimate concerns for Andrea's healing ability and increased risk of infection, especially with injuries.

One such delay was due to Andrea's extreme bruising injury, or subdermal hematoma, caused by punching a window that didn't break. When he saw her hand, the oncologist said she had to delay chemo and ordered her to see a doctor at First Care (a walk-in clinic). Andrea told the doctor at First Care about being fired for being transgender, being diagnosed with polycythemia vera, Stage IV Cancer and a brain aneurysm, so this hand injury was the least of her concerns. In early July 2018, Andrea's hand was healed enough to get cleared for chemo. I took photos of her taking a nap in the nearly empty infusion room with her IV pole - about $20,000 worth of medicine in those little clear bags.

This round of chemo had extra awful side effects. Even with all 4 anti-nausea medications onboard simultaneously, Andrea was terribly nauseous and unable to eat or function anywhere close to normal. When I called and spoke with one of the cancer care nurses about Andrea's blood tests, I expressed concern about the worsening side effects. Then it dawned on me to ask the nurse to look in Andrea's charts to see if maybe they'd changed the dosing of the chemo drugs on that round. Sure enough, they had! She told me that 2 of the chemo drugs had been increased on that infusion WITHOUT TELLING US. There was no discussion of "upping" the meds or warning us to expect extra side effects. Finding that out AFTER THE FACT really pissed me off. Then, I told the nurse the side effects were so bad that Andrea was considering quitting chemo. I asked her, "At what point do you give up on chemo? At what point do you say, 'I can't take this anymore'?" She replied that we'd need to have that discussion with the doctor. Then I asked what other patients do in this situation. She replied that they'd either asked for more days off between treatments or they'd ask for decreased doses of chemo drugs in hopes of lessening the suffering caused by the side effects. Considering that each successive treatment gets worse, doctors have to balance the "good" of an effectively high dose against the severity of increased side effects and what the patient can handle. The goal is to be as aggressive as possible within the patient's tolerance level. Everyone is different, so it's a tricky balance to find. Still, I wished they had actually discussed those things WITH us, rather than making decisions FOR us.

Andrea finished round 7, but they reminded us that they wanted her to do at least 12. She didn't know if she would make it to 12 because the side effects were unbearable. We actually wrote them down. At the time, this was her list of Chemo Side Effects:

1. Peripheral neuropathy
2. Cracking/splitting fingertips
3. Never ending nausea
4. Hair loss
5. "Sun burned" dry skin (face)
6. Wincing in ears
7. Taste buds "off"/nothing tastes right (even water tastes bad)
8. Loss of appetite
9. Sensitivity to cold
10. Extreme fatigue ("chemo crash")
11. Mouth sores (inside)
12. Cracked/painful corners of mouth and nose
13. Port pain
14. Blurred vision
15. Constipation, painful/strained bowel movements (worries about pressure on aneurysm)
16. Anxiety
17. Depression
18. Suicidal ideation
19. Anger/agitation
20. Emotional distress over the ethical dilemma of her treatments making money for Big Pharma and being stuck in a healthcare system that she doesn't agree with but can't change.

Andrea questioned whether her shitty quality of life was still worth living or not. She debated delaying her next treatment an extra week or giving up on chemo altogether. There were just too many side effects. And each round's side effects would get worse and worse (they called this the "cumulative effect"). We wondered: if it was this unbearable now, how would she make it five more rounds?

CHAPTER 3: UPHILL BATTLE

From my view, Andrea's disease was horrible, but the treatment seemed worse. I hoped someday people would look back on chemo in disbelief and horror that we would do something so barbaric without assurance that it would work. The treatment was often worse than the disease it was meant to treat. However, I recognized that only Andrea knew what she could handle and what she was willing to live with, so I always supported her decisions. In late July 2018, after an extra week off from chemo to give herself time to think about what she wanted to do, Andrea decided to start another round. Her reasoning was: If she gave up now, everyone (including her) would be left wondering "what if." What if we'd tried everything we could? Would it have made a difference? Would it have mattered?

Andrea knew her decision involved more pain and suffering because of the chemo side effects, but she felt that her past experiences with pain and suffering had prepared her and given her the ability to cope with this reality. I admired her decision to fight and her ability to endure the pain and suffering; I doubt that I could do the same if I were in her shoes. As we so often debated, the real struggle was between quality of life and quantity of life. For Andrea, if she didn't feel functional at least half of the time, then it wasn't worth it. Functionality fluctuated depending on what point in the treatment cycle she was in. I told her that if the ratio was such that she couldn't endure more suffering, I would respect her decision to discontinue chemo. But she decided to carry on, in hopes that all the fighting would be worth it.

However, Andrea decided NOT to take the new antibiotic they prescribed for her chemo skin rash because the side effects included "nausea," "ringing in the ears," "loss of appetite," and "stomach/abdominal pain" – all of which she had enough of already! But, more importantly, it had rare side effects of causing "a serious increase in pressure inside the skull (intracranial hypertension)" and "a chance of permanent vision loss or blindness." Here's what we wanted to know: Why in the world would they prescribe something that could potentially cause intracranial hypertension in a patient with a known brain aneurysm? Clearly, oncologists aren't experts in brain aneurysms, so they gave her a referral to a neurosurgeon in Anchorage. Andrea said, "It would be pretty sucky to beat cancer only to die of a treatable brain aneurysm," so we started working on the insurance approval and travel arrangements to get it evaluated by the specialist.

In August, five months into chemo, we finally had a breakthrough! After battling the intense nausea all the time (the main source of Andrea's suffering), we finally figured out how to stay on top of it! The trick was NOT to do what the prescription bottle said: "take one tablet at the first sign of nausea." By then it was too late! Instead, take it every six hours REGARDLESS. Day or night, set the timer for 6 hours and take the damn medicine whether you feel nausea or not. That's how you stay ahead of it! This strategy made a WORLD of difference! I had never seen Andrea be able to eat that much during a cycle before! And she didn't lose so much weight as every time before! I sure wished someone would have told us that trick to begin with! It could've saved her so much suffering!

That discovery came just in time, as Andrea's other type of suffering (peripheral nephropathy) was getting worse. It was to the point of unacceptable function loss, so they decided to cut the offending chemo drug for a couple rounds in hopes that her body could heal enough for her to regain some feeling back in her fingertips. One time while Andrea was in the infusion room, I went down the hall in full "patient advocate mode" to talk with the nurse resource navigator. I told her all the ways the system had failed us and all the hurdles we'd faced so far. She was shocked. She couldn't believe how much we'd been through. I told her I just wanted her to know everything in hopes that she could help other patients and caregivers avoid the same pitfalls. She said that, in many ways, we "fell through the cracks." She was also extremely grateful I told her about things we eventually found (the hard way) that helped us because SHE DIDN'T KNOW. Literally, the nurse in charge of helping patients/caregivers navigate resources was UNAWARE of Access Alaska's PCA/DSP program or about applying for Social Security Disability. Here I was informing her about what resources cancer patients need and how we obtained them (much later than we needed them) when we really should've been informed of those resources by someone like her at the very beginning of the treatment journey! She claimed she would use the information I gave her to help other patients and caregivers. Hopefully future people wouldn't have to suffer some of the same things we had. Part of the problem in Fairbanks was that oncology was a private clinic, radiation was a private clinic, the nurse navigator and social worker were hospital staff – and nobody seemed to talk to each other. There seemed to be no comprehensive support or communication. The family/caregiver had to be navigating everything because the patients didn't have the energy to fight the system while they're fighting cancer.

However, I believed the issues were even bigger and deeper than that. At its core, the U.S. healthcare system was designed solely for profits. Money was the only thing that motivated pharmaceutical companies, medical research, and even FDA approvals. And doctors/clinics/hospitals were FORCED to care about profits in order to stay in business. All this meant that the focus was not, could not, be on patient care. It meant patient care, at best, was secondary. Yes, there were amazing nurses who did an amazing job, but above them was a huge corporate system that they could not control. I believed that if we *truly* cared about patients, all healthcare would be not-for-profit. I witnessed first-hand the reasons why we needed universal healthcare.

Near the end of August, another chemo treatment got bumped. The drug that caused neuropathy (Oxaliplatin) was accompanied by a powerful anti-nausea medicine; but without Oxaliplatin, the insurance wouldn't cover the anti-nausea medicine (so we'd have to pay out-of-pocket). Andrea was already nauseous and didn't want more nausea. Also, two hours after her blood draw, they still hadn't started her infusion. The infusion room was packed. They literally didn't have enough chairs for all the patients. Andrea finally refused to do the treatment, and we left. The downside to bumping treatment was that the following cycle would get bumped, too, which put it in conflict with her neurosurgeon appointment in Anchorage. We decided the brain aneurysm was more important to get evaluated, so the following cycle got bumped instead of rescheduling the neurosurgeon.

Meanwhile, the oncologist ordered Andrea another CT scan to see her cancer progression and determine if the chemotherapy was effective or not. But it took me calling the office repeatedly over several days to get the results because only providers are allowed to give results, not office staff. Sick of the phone tag, I drove down to the clinic just to pick up copies of the test results because we didn't want to wait. The results had both good news and bad news. The good news was "no new cancer growth," "unchanged from the previous study." Of course, shrinkage was preferred, but no new growth was still better than growth. The bad news was they discovered a minor aortic aneurysm that wasn't there before. So, it appeared the treatment was keeping the growth under control, but now she had another aneurysm (first one: brain; second one: aorta). My online searches indicated Andrea had several risk factors for aneurysms: former smoker, high BP, coffee drinker, and family history.

Our Anchorage visit to the neurosurgeon was a success and we asked all our questions and got answers regarding our concerns. Basically, we were told that the size, shape, and location of Andrea's brain aneurysm was a relatively low risk, especially when compared to her other health issues. The neurosurgeon was actually more concerned about Andrea getting a referral to a vascular surgeon to evaluate the aortic aneurysm. But we still learned a lot from the neurosurgeon about brain aneurysms, such as: 1) To learn the exact shape, the neurosurgeon could perform a diagnostic angiogram (but the risks of that procedure outweighed the benefits for Andrea); 2) Typically, intervention/treatment isn't needed unless the size increased to 6+mm, or ruptures; 3) There's only a 1% risk of rupture per year for the type of aneurysm that Andrea had; 4) We'd previously been told to avoid anything that could raise her blood pressure, but the neurosurgeon said Andrea could resume all normal everyday activities without restriction; 5) A follow-up MRA was scheduled for 6 months later to see if there was any change over time; 6) It was unknown if having cancer or doing chemo had any effect on her aneurysm. Following the neurosurgeon appointment, we had a talk with the oncologist which resulted in a referral to a vascular surgeon (to assess the aortic aneurysm) and a discussion about length of cancer treatment. Basically, we were told Andrea would continue chemotherapy for as long as she could tolerate the side effects of the chemo drugs. I had a difficult time wrapping my head around Andrea doing chemo the rest of her life.

When anyone asked, I felt I was repeating the same scenario about Andrea's health: still struggling with chemo side effects and not really having solid answers about prognosis. But Andrea kept fighting. Even when she developed side effects like the painful skin cracking (that she'd had on her face and fingers) on her toes. Between chemo fatigue and painful toes, I was surprised she was still walking around the house. I was continually impressed with her will to live and her willingness to continue treatment, despite the constant depression, anxiety, pain, and uncertainty. She had several types of balm for the skin cracking, and they helped, but only if she used them consistently. The lack of consistency was due to "chemo brain" (not being able to remember simple things like taking medicine) and the fact that the slightest touch was painful (so, applying the balm itself, hurt).

In October, a routine dental exam revealed Andrea might have another cancer – in her jaw. There was a clear outline of a cyst/tumor on the X-ray. The dentist was so concerned about it that he referred us to an oral surgeon to have it biopsied. We learned that chemo changes the Ph of your saliva, which disrupts the balance of good and bad bacteria in your mouth, leading to tooth decay. That explained why Andrea's teeth had been chipping and decaying. We also learned that acidic drinks (like coffee, orange juice, wine, all things she loved) made this Ph imbalance worse. The dentist said that while he would like to fix Andrea's decaying teeth, he'd first need written approval from all the other doctors (oncologist, neurosurgeon, vascular surgeon) because the anesthetic used by dentists is too much of a risk for patients with untreated aneurysms. So, all we could do was minimize tooth decay by avoiding acidic drinks, which Andrea was pretty depressed about it. She had so few pleasures left, and they were all slowly taken away.

Fortunately, we got a little good news. When we saw the oral surgeon, he first took a CBCT (3D x-ray), then he decided not to biopsy her jaw because he already knew what it was! The surgeon wrote in his report, "The lesion is radiographically and clinically consistent with a Stafne bone defect. The radiolucency is caused by a lingual mandibular salivary gland depression. No additional surgical intervention is necessary." Basically, that meant it was nothing to worry about and Andrea was cleared to resume chemo. Andrea was relieved that she didn't have to get her face/jaw cut open for a biopsy. Next, we saw the vascular surgeon and he said no surgery was required because Andrea's aortic aneurysm was relatively small and not a threat unless it got bigger. He said he'd keep an eye on it with the CT scans used to monitor her cancer, but he was concerned that her cancer was significantly more life-threatening than her aortic aneurysm.

Meanwhile, Andrea's eye lashes were itching and growing like crazy! A strange side effect of one of the chemo drugs was that the hair on the head thins, but everything else grows! Even the areas of her body that completed laser hair removal all grew back while she was on chemo. The chemo nurses said a couple other patients had this happen – to the point that trimming was necessary because of impaired eyesight. We'd already trimmed Andrea's lashes, but she got nervous with a pair of scissors that close to her eye. So, she mostly used an eye lash curler to curl them up out of her vision. We eventually used a pair of snub-nosed scissors made for dog groomers to trim safely around eyes. People made comments about how long they were – or wrongly assumed they were extensions!

However, by far, the worst side effects were from Oxalyplatin, the chemo drug that caused extreme cold sensitivity. In my opinion, it was inhumane to force Andrea to stay in Alaska all winter. The pain and suffering were just too much for her to tolerate. To lessen her suffering, we decided to seek treatment in Seattle at Swedish Cancer Institute for a few months during the coldest part of the winter. Because insurance wouldn't pay for travel or accommodations, I had to start a GoFundMe campaign to help cover the cost of getting us to Seattle and the higher cost of living there. Fortunately, two friends donated their airline miles and other friends donated just enough to hold the reservation on the Airbnb. Andrea's friend Sarah agreed to let us borrow her car while we were in Seattle so we could make the drive from the Airbnb to the hospital for treatments. After I explained the reason for our stay in Seattle, the owner of the Airbnb was kind enough to give us a discount. In many ways, we were very fortunate that people were willing to help.

When people asked, "Why Seattle?" I'd explain that Fairbanks wasn't exactly on the cutting edge for specialized medical treatment, and there were several big factors that really influenced Andrea's decision to seek treatment in Seattle: 1) Swedish Cancer Institute had an expert who specialized in colon cancer (Dr. Gold) and comprehensive care that Fairbanks simply didn't offer; 2) Seattle had a less harsh winter than Fairbanks, and given Andrea's extreme cold sensitivity, staying in Fairbanks meant an unacceptable level of pain and suffering; 3) Washington is a legal Death With Dignity state, which Andrea wanted to establish connections with because that option offered what she believed she had the right to choose for herself; and 4) Seattle was vegan-friendly, cannabis-friendly, and LGBTQ-friendly. For me, the icing on the cake was that I could continue to do both my jobs, as Andrea's PCA/DSP and doing data analysis, while in Seattle. For Andrea, the icing on the cake was that her adorable companion of 20 years, Tigerlilly, officially became her emotional support animal. I started training Tigerlilly to travel in the car so she would be ready to go to Seattle with us. Tigerlilly had become even more attached and attentive since Andrea started chemo (and she continued to be an absolute sweetheart during our time in Seattle).

Oftentimes, Andrea's "chemo crash" came on immediately upon clearing the front door. The first couple days following pump removal, Andrea experienced "fall out," often a face-plant onto the couch (usually with a kitty cat nearby). Sometimes Andrea warned me that she was about to crash. She'd have slurred speech and deliriously mumble something about just needing a "power nap," then zonk for hours at a time, later waking up asking what year it was or who the president was. I would love nothing more than to tell her Trump wasn't president, but I couldn't lie.

In November, we saw a visiting oncologist who bragged to us about how he'd practiced medicine for 30 years. I asked if I could pick his brain about what exactly we were looking at with Andrea's situation. His answer: "If you take 100 people with metastatic disease and follow them through 5 years of treatment, about half of them will still be with us." At the time, I thought he was implying that Andrea had a 50% chance of living through 5 years of treatment. But, as I thought about it over the following week, I realized he hadn't actually told us anything meaningful. For example, he'd lumped 100 people with metastatic disease all together without regard for either the stage of that disease nor the part of the body that disease was in. Were these 100 people diagnosed at Stage I, II, III, IV? Was the disease in the liver, lungs, brain, where? And, at what point did they begin treatment? If he'd actually answered my question, he would've said, "If you take 100 people in Andrea's age range with Stage IV colon cancer...." I started to see that doctors either can't or won't tell you what you want to know. I'm relatively well educated, so it made me wonder how the hell the average citizen navigates the healthcare system. So many barriers and hoops to jump through! It's often a full-time job just being a patient advocate for someone needing serious medical treatment. What if somebody didn't have anyone advocating for them? It made me grateful I could be that advocate for Andrea, but I worried about people less fortunate.

There were a lot of frustrating days fighting the system in preparation for our trip to Seattle. The once helpful social worker at Swedish decided she wanted nothing to do with us, the doctor's office there claimed that the Fairbanks oncologist had no knowledge of us going to Seattle (even though we'd discussed it multiple times), they refused to book an appointment with the Swedish oncologist until Andrea had another CT scan, and they wouldn't book her infusion appointment until they had insurance pre-authorization (the alternative was paying $30,000 out-of-pocket). I was also trying to get Andrea's medications authorized for Seattle, pack for the 3-month trip, get the house ready to freeze, and attend a court hearing to have PCA/DPS services authorized for her doctor appointments, infusions, and blood draws in Seattle. Being a patient advocate was a full-time job. The hoops I had to jump through to get proper care for Andrea seemed excessive.

Andrea did her last Fairbanks infusion on New Years Eve. Our friends came up from Anchorage to spend a few days with us before we left for Seattle. They brought Andrea some fun hats and NYE accessories to dress up in the infusion room and we had our own little house party that evening. Before cancer, we would've dressed up and gone out to a big NYE party, probably at a bar. After cancer, we had small at-home parties, most of which while she was tethered to that despised portable infusion pump.

January temperatures were the reason Andrea was excited to go to Seattle. It was about 75 degrees warmer! She was so miserable in the Alaska cold (the chemo side effects made it so painful) especially since the motor in our pellet stove died. We winterized the house, packed up, and finally got on a plane with Tigerlilly (she was a perfect travel companion for Andrea). We landed in Seattle thanks to so many people who helped us make it possible. We couldn't have done it without that support. I will always be grateful to friends and family who loved Andrea enough to help out in any way they could. The first part of being in Seattle was all about cat naps and sweet kitty snuggles. Tigerlilly watched over Andrea, slept with her, gave slow blinks and head bumps. She was such a sweetheart! She traveled like a pro and adjusted to being in Seattle with no problems at all. I was so impressed with her bond to Andrea and how easily she adapted to our life changes.

However, our first appointment in Seattle felt like a bomb dropped. We finally got some expert answers, but they were NOT the answers we wanted to hear. Dr. Gold (oncologist at Swedish Cancer Institute and expert in colon cancer) was straight forward with his answers to my questions (I came prepared with a list). I told him it was no exaggeration to say that Andrea's diagnosis and subsequent treatment had completely changed our lives. He agreed. His exact words were, "Yes, it turns everything upside down." My main concern was making sure Andrea had some kind of quality of life (which was difficult to do on chemo). I asked if there were any other treatment options we should consider. He said, "No. Just keep doing chemo." I asked if she would be a candidate for any trials. He said, "No, not unless chemo stops controlling the cancer growth." He said, "The other option is to quit chemo and let nature take its course." When I asked about prognosis and life expectancy, he reminded us that her disease was not curable and that we would be dealing with this the rest of her life (however long that might be) and that chemo was only a method to "kick the can down the road as far as you can, for as long as you can." I said we needed to know how long we had left, so that we could plan appropriately. He said that, clinically, with cases like Andrea, life expectancy was based off the date of diagnosis and that the median is 29 months. This meant that 50% of patients like Andrea survived 29 months after diagnosis, and 50% didn't. Also, this was assuming they were doing chemo the whole time. At that point, it had been 12 months since Andrea was diagnosed, so that meant 17 months were left before she hit the 29-month median. There were patients who lived past the median, but the percentages were lower and lower each month. According to the American Cancer Society's website, for Stage IV colorectal cancer, the survival rate after 5 years of chemo was only 10%. "But" I said, "most of those people are much older than Andrea. Surely her relatively young age gives her an advantage, right?" "No," the doctor said, "age doesn't matter." Up till that point, I thought her relatively young age was her biggest advantage; it turned out to be inconsequential. That was when reality set in. Basically, Andrea had roughly 17 months left (assuming she continued to do chemo) and her age was not an advantage. This was devastating. I was incapable of wrapping my head around it.

Given the awful side effects of chemo, I wanted to discuss quality of life issues. I'd been keeping a full list of Andrea's side effects, which I offered to show the doctor, but he refused, saying, "None of it would surprise me." He wouldn't even look at my list of over 30 side effects I'd been tracking. We only discussed the biggest offenders (difficult and painful bowel movements, peripheral nephropathy, and extreme cold sensitivity). I especially wanted to know how long the cold sensitivity would last – because I needed to know if we should leave Alaska permanently. He said the chemo drug that caused the cold sensitivity was the same one that caused the peripheral nephropathy (Oxaliplatin), which had a half-life of 50 days, where the symptoms got worse before they got better, and that it took at least 3 months after cutting the drug to start regaining some normalcy. Because of the severity of Andrea's peripheral nephropathy, they discontinued the Oxaliplatin a couple cycles before Seattle, but it would be reintroduced if her CT scans show any growth (which would inevitably happen). This made me question her viability in Alaska, especially during the winter. Would we escape to Seattle EVERY winter? If she only had 17 months left, why spend it being cold and miserable while dealing with a list of literally 32 other side effects?

When trying to express myself to others during this time, I'd attempt to type out a Facebook message or email, and I'd end up erasing a whole bunch of "F" words and other profanities expressing how I felt about cancer, chemo, and the destruction of our hopes and dreams together. We had worked so hard to build our house; we thought we would grow old there together. It was impossible to accept that 17 months was all we had left. And, that time would undoubtedly be filled with more pain and suffering. All I wanted to do was flee to a tropical beach, so at least she could be warm and happy during her last months. But we were forced to choose between Alaska and Washington state because her insurance was Alaska Medicaid. At least both states had legal cannabis. Cannabis was the only reason Andrea was able to stay off narcotics and opiates (that the doctors constantly wanted to prescribe to her). However, if we'd had the money, we definitely would've had more treatment options in other states or other countries. As it was, we had to use GoFundMe just to get to Seattle. And, as much as we wanted to, we couldn't get legally married or else I wouldn't be allowed to be her PCA/DSP (which was helping pay the bills) and she'd lose part of her disability benefits. We just couldn't afford to do anything she really wanted.

CHAPTER 4: FEAR AND
LOATHING IN LAS INSURANCE

It took A LOT of effort to get us to Seattle, but finally, Andrea's first day of chemo at Swedish Cancer Institute happened in January 2019. We had issues waiting for insurance approval (funny how they'll pay $45,000/month for chemo drugs, but not $18 for anti-nausea meds). By far, Andrea's favorite part was that Swedish routinely offered Lidocaine to numb the port before jamming the needle into her chest. Receiving treatment at Swedish was the only time she had her port accessed for chemo without pain.

We settled into our little Seattle Airbnb, started her Swedish chemo schedule, and I continued working remotely. However, after 30 days, Alaska Medicaid denied Andrea's PCA/DSP services (that I got paid to provide) for the duration of our Seattle stay. We panicked. We seriously thought we'd be forced to change our plane tickets and go home early because we couldn't afford the loss. But, in February, Andrea's friend surprised us with a bank transfer and saved us from having to make that tough decision! The friend explained it this way: "One should not have to decide between obtaining care or not. Our medical system is broken. While I had no prior knowledge of the difficult choices you two were facing prior to offering help, I am glad I was able to do so. Often times things line up as they are intended, call it God providing or the stars aligning, who knows. We are all in this thing called life together;

we must all do our part to make another's life more enjoyable and less distraught with these choices."

On Andrea's 3rd chemo cycle in Seattle, I attended the Caregivers Support Group and Dr. Gold agreed to write a letter to help support Andrea's appeal for Medicaid to continue to cover her PCA/DSP services while at Swedish (which, unfortunately, they still denied). Among other caregivers, I met a woman from Canada at the support group who was a caregiver to a family member receiving treatment at Swedish. When I said that I believed it's immoral/unethical to make profit off sick and dying people, she said "That's your Canadian talking." I couldn't tell if that was an insult or a compliment, but I took it as AT LEAST an acknowledgment that I wasn't the only person who took issue with the U.S. healthcare system.

In March 2019, Andrea completed her 20th chemo cycle. TWENTY. I remember being so surprised that she had made it that far because the original oncologist just wanted her to try and get to twelve! I was continually amazed by Andrea's strength to keep fighting even when she was suffering. But it was a team effort; neither of us would have fought without the other. As a friend remarked, "Commitment and love makes the unbearable manageable." Indeed, Andrea had even declared what she called her FIGHT SONG, "Rise Up" by Andra Day, which some of our dear friends sang in the Fairbanks Rainbow Choir a month later; I don't think there was a dry eye in the whole building.

As we prepared to leave Seattle, I realized Andrea hadn't touched her guitar once. We'd paid extra baggage fees to have one of her favorite guitars transported on the plane because she couldn't bear the thought of not being able to make music for 3 months. But due to the side effects of chemo, she was incapable of playing. Considering she had been playing guitar regularly since age 15, this was a drastic change and a big loss of something she loved. It would be almost another year later before the peripheral neuropathy eased enough for her to feel the strings enough to play guitar again.

Since Dr. Gold had made it clear that her remaining time was limited, Andrea wanted to learn more details about Washington state's Death With Dignity laws. So, I called the office for End of Life Washington; their motto is "Your life. Your death. Your choice." I explained that we were in Seattle for cancer treatment, that we were seeking information, and that we had questions regarding their process. The woman answering my call was very kind and willing to answer all our inquiries; she said we were asking all the right questions. She explained the paperwork involved and emailed a packet for us to read and forms to fill out. We told her that our friends from Alaska had recently completed the process in Washington and that we wished to do the same. She explained that the law only applied to Washington residents, but that there were ways of getting around it, as our friends had done. Andrea made it clear that she wanted the choice and the control over WHERE and WHEN to end her fight with cancer. End of Life Washington provided the HOW. Understanding the process and requirements for choosing Death With Dignity gave us both a lot of peace. It was a comfort just knowing that Andrea had a plan for when the time came.

Although we were only in Seattle for 3 months, it was precious time together. Just us – and sweet Tigerlilly. Turns out, a 20-year-old kitty has about the same energy as a cancer patient. Tigerlilly and Andrea took lots of cat naps together while I worked on my laptop. Our little Airbnb was tiny: a bedroom, kitchen, dining room, and living room – all in one room. It was about a 20-minute drive from Swedish Cancer Institute. There were beautiful parks within walking distance, but I only succeeded in getting Andrea out for a walk once – and she struggled the entire time. I was reluctant to leave her unattended, so I rarely left the Airbnb without her. Our world seemed a little smaller, but I loved the time we had together and the few outings (besides the hospital) that she was able to tolerate.

Just prior to her last treatment at Swedish, Dr. Gold ordered another CT scan (which, again, we had to fight insurance for) and a follow-up MRA was scheduled in Fairbanks to check on her brain aneurysm. The CT results of Andrea's chest/abdomen/pelvis showed relatively small changes. The omental nodularity had slightly decreased, but the peritoneal nodules had increased (up to 11mm). Two new developments included a growing nodule in the left lobe of her lungs (it was unknown if it was cancerous or not, but it measured 4x9mm) and thickening of her bladder wall (as if it were infected, but she had no urinary symptoms - yet). Dr. Gold ordered extra Granix injections for the last chemo round in Seattle, which was good because Andrea's immune system needed the boost for traveling back to Alaska and being around people/germs in airports and airplanes. Dr. Gold recommended we continue chemo as usual in Fairbanks and monitor everything via CT again in another couple months. So, we headed home grateful and hopeful, but Andrea really struggled with traveling. Physically, she just couldn't handle the rigors of airports. I realized she'd probably never again make the trip back to Seattle, and unfortunately, I was right.

We had a very rough first week back in Fairbanks. In our absence, despite our preparations, our house had frozen and thawed. The damage forced us to replace the water heater, the washing machine, all the food in the fridge/freezer, and the blower motor in the pellet stove. Worst of all, our kitty Tigerlilly had 3 infections requiring vet visits. Once again, our beloved friends came to the rescue. Each of those catastrophes was paid for by a different friend. We were so very thankful. We seriously wouldn't have been able to deal with all those expenses without our incredibly generous and loving friends. Andrea's birthday was shortly thereafter, and our friends once again came out in support by sending her flowers, gifts, sweets, cards, food, wine, and loving messages.

Those precious moments of kindness were in such stark contrast to the relentless struggle with cancer. I especially loathed insurance. It was a constant battle over what treatments/medications they would or wouldn't cover – and the rules were always changing. For weeks after arriving home, I had been trying to get refills for one of Andrea's important anti-nausea drugs, but insurance stopped covering it. The prescribing doctor sent multiple requests for authorization, to no avail. Knowing how badly Andrea needed it, I finally gave up and paid out-of-pocket ($23 each). Unfortunately, the drug (scopolamine) took 12 hours to take effect, and I was too late; the nausea got really bad after they pulled her portable infusion pump, and she spent all night throwing up. Call me crazy, but I think that if you're already fighting cancer, you shouldn't have to also fight insurance to get the meds your doctor prescribes. Sometimes it felt like they almost wanted patients to give up and die. The U.S. system is geared toward making money, not people's health. One of my Canadian relatives was confused, asking "Why did you file bankruptcy and start a GoFundMe because of cancer?" Exhausted, all I could muster in reply was, "Because it's the American healthcare system."

As is often the case with many things, place matters. For instance, Andrea's chemo treatment in Seattle was only $15,000/month (as compared to $45,000/month in Fairbanks). So, by staying in Seattle for 3 months, we saved the insurance a total of $90,000. The least they could do is cover her $23 anti-nausea medication! Healthcare in Alaska is just plain expensive. In many cases, it's cheaper to fly patients out of state. High overhead, high cost of living, high shipping costs, and high doctor salaries all contribute to Alaska's high healthcare expenses. Andrea's Fairbanks oncologist told us about a patient he treated who had an easy-to-treat kind of cancer that only required an oral chemo pill. But the patient's insurance refused to cover it ($4,000/month). Rather than continuing to fight the insurance, the patient decided to give up and die. THAT was the story the doctor told us in response to our complaining that Andrea's insurance refused to cover one of her anti-nausea meds. The insurance industry is corrupt, unethical, purely profit-driven, and makes it difficult (or impossible) for doctors to do their job for their patients. Andrea's oncologist knew she could only take a couple kinds of anti-nausea drugs because most of them interfered with other perscription drugs she was on. This is why we couldn't switch to a different one when the insurance decided to stop covering the drug she'd been taking. At one point, the frustrated doctor said, "Okay, fine, so the insurance won't cover the $23 drug? Then I'll just give you the $700 IV anti-nausea drug instead. See how they like that."

I often hesitated to write updates on Andrea's cancer page because it seemed like I complained a lot and I thought people might get tired of it. But thankfully, friends reminded me that everyone on that page cared about Andrea and that my posts were also a window into the cancer business, insurance racket, and healthcare system in America that people learned about via those updates. After 3.5 weeks of fighting and getting the runaround (with doctor's office, pharmacy, and insurance all blaming each other), there was a collective cheer when I FINALLY picked up Andrea's scopolamine. Friends called me a "badass." But I HAD to be a badass for Andrea's sake. When she was 'chemo crashed,' there was simply no way she was capable of fighting the system.

Just as we celebrated one small victory, another battle would begin. The next one required the doctor to fight the insurance once again. They required her oncologist to "prove the need for and justify the use of an infuser" to administer Andrea's chemotherapy drugs. Those infusion machines are required for every IV chemo patient to receive their treatments. But insurance forced the provider to jump through a bunch of ridiculous hoops so that Andrea could just continue receiving the same treatments that insurance had already approved for over a year. It was so maddening that the provider claimed that he "went into a cussing tirade like a drunken sailor" while on the phone with insurance representatives. I responded, "Oh good, it's not just me!"

By June 2019, Andrea chose to cancel a treatment so she could be functional for Pride Fest. She was running the sound booth as their sound engineer AND donated all her equipment to the event. That was a big deal for multiple reasons: 1) she was almost never social, but having "a job" to do got her out of the house, 2) Fairbanks hadn't had a Pride celebration on that scale in 25 years, and 3) the last cycle's side effects were so brutal that she definitely deserved a break for a couple weeks to recover, be functional, and gain back some weight. It turned out that skipping a chemo treatment worked beautifully for Andrea's functionality level and she was able to kick ass during Pride Fest as the sound engineer. I was amazed by her level of function on chemo versus off chemo; it was like night and day. During that brief break in treatment, I saw glimpses of the person I fell in love with! It was surprising how much of the person I loved got masked by side effects when she was on chemo. As much as I preferred that she not endure all the bullshit of more chemo, we had to go back to the Cancer Center for her infusion treatment after the Pride event. We also discussed the bladder pain and UTI-like symptoms Andrea had been having over the previous month. Her doctor ordered another CT scan to compare to the one in Seattle that showed thickening of the bladder wall. In the meantime, we began yet another battle with insurance. They began to require "prior authorization" for every prescription refill. Not just new prescriptions, but all refills, every time. This was super annoying because they didn't warn us of this policy change ahead of time. So, I showed up at the pharmacy to get the medicine only to find out I had to pay out-of-pocket because the "prior authorization" either wasn't requested or not completed. It was just another strategy that helped insurance to avoid paying. When people are desperate for their medicine and are already standing in the pharmacy, what are the chances they'll walk away and wait a couple more days for the "prior authorization" to go through?

As we were on our way to the hospital for the CT scan, Andrea got a telemarketer call trying to sell a home cancer testing kit. She interrupted the salesperson to say she already had Stage IV cancer. The salesperson continued with the sales script anyway. Again, Andrea explained she didn't need a home cancer testing kit because she already knew she had cancer, that we were literally enroute to the hospital. The salesperson said "oh, whatever" and hung up. I didn't know whether to laugh or cry. We found out later that the call was likely one of the many scams used to get patient's Medicaid/Medicare ID numbers for fraudulent purposes (Medicaid is for the poor or disabled, and Medicare is for the elderly); there seemed to be no limit to the ways in which the system tries to screw the vulnerable.

After Andrea's all-day treatments, then being sent home with a new kind of portable infusion pump that she really disliked, we were overwhelmed with the overall unpleasant feelings we had been dealing with. Fortunately, our friend put on her nurse's hat and recommended ideas for coping, asking for help, self-care, support, and insisted we get an appointment with Palliative Care. We scheduled a consultation and hoped they could help us manage all the struggles that came with the cancer business. After 16 months of chemo, we were exhausted. The chemo crashes were getting worse. Extreme fatigue and nausea (even with multiple meds on board) made life hard to live. After 40 hours on the couch, in a near-coma-like state, Andrea would finally, barely, eat a piece of toast.

Before we could see the Palliative Care doctor, we saw the oncologist to get the new CT scan results which showed no significant changes. No shrinking, but no growing. The treatments appeared to be "pausing" the cancer growth, but not reducing it. Bladder thickening and nodules in lungs also were not significantly changed. Although Andrea was supposed to do chemo following her CT results, her blood counts were too low, and the doctor said she had to skip a week and try again the next week. We were happy about taking a break because the last treatment had such horrible side effects that they made her want to quit chemo altogether.

By August 2019, our friends had decided that due to Andrea's limited survival time, she needed to determine what was most important to her to do – before she could no longer do it. So, at the insistence of these friends, I asked Andrea, "If you could do ANYTHING before you die, what would it be?" She replied, "I'd want to go back to Kauai." Once her answer was relayed to her friends, they started planning, raising funds, and collaborating. Thanks to the extreme generosity of these super amazing people, they told us that we were going to Kauai in December! Turned out, some kind friends donated their Marriott points to book us 6 days lodging, and some other friends donated their Alaska Airlines miles to book our flights! Andrea was in disbelief. She was amazed that anyone cared about her enough to grant her a last wish. It almost felt like one of those clips from Make-A-Wish Foundation. Now we just had to CROSS OUR FINGERS that Andrea was going to be healthy enough to travel. We started making a gameplan by working with her oncologist to give her a break from chemo starting around Thanksgiving so she could *hopefully* feel well enough to enjoy the trip. The best bonus: Andrea's daughter and her then-boyfriend were going to be coming to Kauai with us, too!

Around this time, we also received some much needed help from The Interior Alaska Cancer Association with paying a few basic bills (food and utilities). They relied solely on donations to help people dealing with cancer, so many of our friends, family, and neighbors had donated. It truly takes an entire community to meet the needs of the vulnerable in our society, which is why civilized nations created universal healthcare systems decades ago. But people in the U.S. are still forced to piece together their care by petitioning to this program or that program, applying to this agency or that agency, crowdsourcing online, posting on social media, writing to lawmakers and begging drug companies for mercy when friends/family inevitably get tapped out. For patients who don't have friends/family they can rely on, especially if they have a debilitating diagnosis, there's nobody to do the petitioning, applying, posting, writing, begging, or advocating. Indeed, Andrea often told me how lucky she was to have a support network that many other people lack.

During Andrea's next infusion, the Palliative Care doctor finally came to talk with us. Among other things, he asked what goals Andrea wanted to work toward. She answered that there were two:

1) going to Kauai in December, and 2) living to see Trump out of office. The doctor replied, "Well, we ALL want that. Those are good goals." Then he asked what symptoms and side effects he could help us manage so we could meet those goals. We described the biggest offenders (nausea, constipation, extreme fatigue, no appetite). He suggested some new things to try (probiotics, stool softeners, laxatives), so I bought some and we tried them. They made all the difference in the world! Compared to her previous chemo cycle, it was like night and day! I'd never seen her sail through a "chemo crash" so well. Ironically, I was the one that got sick instead! I spent a couple weeks fighting off a cold, but it was the infected lymph nodes that sent me to the doctor. After a round of antibiotics, I started getting better. This was a lesson for me: I had to stay healthy enough to take care of my partner. As we learned just a few months later, all of these key points became even more important. Traveling, trying to stay healthy, taking care of loved ones, and Trump – all played major roles in the pandemic we never saw coming.

CHAPTER 5: CALM BEFORE THE STORM

There's a lot of juggling and trial-and-error to figure out what works in the business of cancer treatment – and management of the resulting side effects. Everyone is different, so there's no "one way" to do it. The Palliative Care doctor explained that because of the nature of her colon cancer, Andrea needed multiple avenues for laxatives to work. Especially with her taking so many anti-nausea drugs both orally and in the infusions that compounded the constipation affect (which would've been worse if she'd taken the prescribed painkillers). To counteract that effect, we had to pursue all avenues. Some laxatives are stimulants that stimulate the bowels to move stool. Others are osmotic that help retain water in the bowel to keep stool soft. The "magic" formula for Andrea seemed to be: 3 Senna the morning of the first day of infusion, then 3 Colace and 1 "Calm" packet with 1 cupful of Mirlax each night of infusion. After 3 days of infusion, she stepped down to just 1-2 Colace per night. She took the probiotic every day regardless of infusion. It took us 17 months of treatment to figure that out! On the one hand, we were glad to finally find a combination of things that helped. But on the other hand, we wished none of it was necessary. As we struggled and figured things out, I often explained them in my update posts on Andrea's cancer page. One friend remarked, "You should write a book about your experiences to help people in the future. Like, chemo tips and social support structures." Indeed, several friends made similar comments. So, when I finally wrote this book about Andrea's journey, I decided to include those kinds of things in hopes they might help others.

By September 2019, we were in need of additional supports. I was still working two jobs and Andrea was still receiving disability benefits, but it just wasn't enough to make ends meet. Thankfully, when we reached out for help, our community did not disappoint. A volunteer with the Interior Alaska Cancer Association petitioned on our behalf with the local credit union and they donated funds to pay part of our property taxes so we wouldn't lose our house. Several friends chipped in with food, firewood, and heating fuel in preparation for winter. We were very fortunate to have such an amazing support system. Even our Facebook friends wrote kind words of love and encouragement when commenting on the updates I posted. Sometimes those updates were hard for me because of the emotional labor and mental where-with-all required to write them. Yes, they were intended to keep friends/family updated, but they were also a way for me to process things and to vent. Later, the posts served as journal entries of sorts, a log of Andrea's journey, and a record of our everyday lives together.

As the fall weather started cooling into winter, a routine blood test showed Andrea's white blood cell counts were low and she was advised to stay away from people to avoid germs. As we were leaving the Cancer Center after infusions, we ran into her old coworker in the parking lot. Until that moment, neither knew each other had cancer. They exchanged their cancer stories and experiences. I was struck by how similar they were. Then, another rough week followed as she was chemo crashed most of the time. She didn't feel well enough to attend a show I performed in. Sadly, she remarked, "I guess I have to get used to missing everything." And it wasn't just chemo side effects; she was also dealing with bladder/urinary pain and the painful port stitches poking through her skin. When she was in her "off week," I tried to get her to come see a movie with me because we hadn't been to a movie theater together in 10 years, but she said she had no tolerance for "people-ing." A friend at the theater asked me how Andrea was doing, and I had to fight back the automatic tears and attempt to formulate a sentence to answer the question. I cannot recall the exact words I used, but it was something to the effect of "cancer is a bitch, and I hate what it's done to the person I love."

Of course, Andrea had her own perspective and opinion on things, which, to me, seemed to be more accepting of her situation. While I often complained about the injustice and unfairness of it all, she always found the "silver linings" and expressed gratitude. She suggested that we focus on thanking people, even acknowledging the little things. One example of this was her request that I write an e-mail to thank the hospital cafeteria staff for providing the opportunity or our lunch dates that we looked forward to when at the Cancer Center for her treatments.

Although we didn't know it, Andrea was just 8 months away from becoming a hospice patient. Treatments were becoming harder and harder for her to tolerate as the side effects intensified over time due to chemo toxicity. She had very painful mouth and tongue sores. We tried several OTC and prescription numbing products, but they provided only mediocre relief for a few moments. It was too painful for her to eat, drink, swallow, or talk. That meant very little food/water intake, resulting in weight loss and no energy. The Cancer Center said she was at risk for dehydration and infection. If it got worse, I was instructed to take her to the ER. Because there was no way she would be well enough nor weigh enough by her next scheduled infusion, we knew she would have to skip another week of treatment. But we saw the doctor anyway and got her labs done to see if her white blood cell count had improved. Andrea told the doctor that if she'd had those painful mouth sores on every cycle, she would have quit chemo already. Fortunately, a Facebook friend said they'd worked with an amazing naturopath who helped their family member mitigate chemo side effects and recommended a mouth swish to combat the mouth sores – and even ordered the ingredients to be delivered to us!

In October, the doctor decided to dial down one of the chemo drugs in her infusion with hopes of reducing some side effects, and it worked! For the first time in years, Andrea felt well enough to leave the house – purely for a social event! In public! With people! That was a BIG DEAL for her! We went to a Halloween party dressed as twin bubble bees! I thought she was so beeeeeeeeeeeautiful! Andrea's daughter said, "DADDIO, YOU ARE THE CUTEST GATDAMN BEE I HAVE EVER SEEN!" And all our friends were so happy for us! Our friends met us at the party, and we were just so grateful for that small miracle. It was Andrea's last Halloween.

In December 2019, it had been 2 years since diagnosis and Andrea had completed 20 months of chemo! Although they dialed down one of the chemo drugs to lessen the horrible side effects, she was still battling the nausea, fatigue, and skin issues. She still had some cold sensitivity, but her skin became most reactive to water. She couldn't take a shower more than once a week – and when she did, her entire body broke out into a red itchy rash. I was concerned about how her skin would react to the water in Kauai (saltwater ocean or chlorinated pools). But I was hoping the little break from chemo would help so that she could actually enjoy the week in Kauai. It would be Andrea's one and only trip with her daughter.

The day before leaving, we went to the vet because things didn't seem right with our kitty. Unfortunately, we had to make the painful decision to say goodbye to our dear sweet Tigerlilly. She was Andrea's emotional support animal and faithful companion for 20 years. She lived a long kitty life, full of love and snuggles. The vet said it was unlikely she'd recover from kidney failure, and we didn't want her to suffer anymore. Our hearts were broken and grieving, but we were grateful to be with her during her final moments rather than her passing while we were gone on the trip (which would've also been traumatic for the petsitter). Later, Andrea requested that Tigerlilly's ashes be mixed with her own and be scattered in the Pacific Ocean.

At long last, we arrived at the airport for Andrea's second and final vacation – and the only trip she ever had with her daughter. So many friends had pitched in to make that last wish come true for her. Although we didn't know it, that trip was just 2 months before COVID shut down the world, and only 10 months before Andrea died. I don't think we could have picked a better time to go. At the time, we just thought Kauai in December was a nice time to leave Alaska and we knew the statistics indicated Andrea had less than a year to live. I was worried that she wouldn't be well enough to travel or enjoy anything, but the break from chemo gave her just enough time to gather her strength. She was able to tolerate short sightseeing outings, little hikes, restaurant dinners, and sitting on the beach. It was rough losing Andrea's emotional support kitty the day before we left on the trip; it felt like we had clouds hanging over us the whole time because we were grieving. We did our best to enjoy being in Kauai, but we were very much mourning the loss of Tigerlilly. And then coming back to Alaska – a one-hundred-degree difference – was just rude! But we truly appreciated everyone's condolences, support, and help in making our Kauai trip possible. It was literally a once-in-a-lifetime vacation.

As expected, we returned to learn that Andrea's CT results showed significant disease progression. We weren't surprised because of her increased symptoms (abdominal pain, lack of appetite, and noticeable hard mass growth in the lower left side of her abdomen). Since the previous treatment was not controlling the cancer anymore, her infusions started including a new drug: Irinotecan/Camptosar. So, then we had a new list of side effects to manage. Incidentally, this addition coincided with a visiting oncologist who went on a rant about how his practice in the lower 48 had been forced to close because insurance companies and government programs (Medicare and Medicaid) only paid 50%-80% of his cost. He was understandably angry that he couldn't cover his costs, while insurance/Medicare/Medicaid imposed limits, restrictions, and regulations that made it both time consuming and difficult to provide appropriate care for his patients. He said he had to battle paperwork and non-medically trained insurance "gatekeepers" who denied approvals and kept treatment out of reach for patients – and made doctors incredibly frustrated. He said the overall system made it nearly impossible for doctors to do their jobs effectively – and patients suffered as a result.

In January 2020, we entered a strange in-between stage. We didn't know if we were preparing for "the inevitable" or for some kind of miracle. So, strangely enough, we were essentially planning for both. That sounded weird, but since there were no guarantees of anything, we just tried to navigate the best we could, given the circumstances. The month prior, we had accomplished 4 major steps: 1) updated/finalized legal paperwork for both of us (Advanced Healthcare Directive, Last Will and Testament, Power of Attorney), 2) met with the funeral home twice, along with the Certified End of Life Doula, 3) began preparations for Andrea's Celebration of Life event, and 4) took our last trip. Combined, these 4 accomplishments helped us feel more prepared (and less stressed) in case the doctors were right about the 29-month median and/ or Andrea couldn't handle the chemo side effects anymore. On the other hand, because she felt she had nothing left to lose, Andrea decided to start an alternative/experimental treatment alongside the conventional treatment. The new alternative/experimental treatment involved a combination of CBD, Vit E, and Fenbendazole. It sounded crazy, but some people had reported success with it. Honestly, it was kind of a "Hail Mary" because it wasn't proven and there was no guarantee she'd have the results others had. But at least it was cheap, accessible, and had no side effects – none of which we could say about chemo. She'd been taking the alternative/experimental treatment since Christmas, but we wouldn't know the results until her next CT scan in April, which coincidentally, was the same time she would hit the 29-month median (when the doctor said half the people with her diagnosis would no longer be with us). Navigating all of the decisions about life and death were very challenging for us. Neither of us had any prior experience. We were so grateful for the love and support that many friends offered as we tiptoed into an uncertain future. But none of us predicted or prepared for what was already brewing in Wuhan, nor how it would ultimately impact Andrea's choices regarding her own death.

CHAPTER 6: EYE OF THE STORM

Some people have an affinity for water, but Andrea had an affinity for fire. She loved having a wood burning stove, chopping wood, building fires, sitting by the fire watching the flames and getting warm. However, nearly 2 years of chemo had impacted every cell in her body. Her physical abilities weren't what they used to be. At the beginning of 2020, Andrea accidentally chopped her thumb while using a hatchet to cut kindling for the wood stove. She was supposed to do chemo two days later, but the doctor decided to defer treatment for a week because of her injury and the risk of infection. Cancer and chemo both weaken the immune system, so oncologists often treat minor injuries as significant infection risks. This meant she got a week off instead of being chemo crashed all week. Still, I banned her from using the hatchet and I started cutting wood to size using the chop saw. Andrea had a high pain tolerance, but she nearly passed out from the pain, as fingertips have so many nerve endings.

In February, Andrea's thumb injury had healed quite nicely, and she completed her 4th infusion with the new chemo drug (Irinotecan/Camptosar). But she was disappointed that she didn't get the diarrhea she was promised as a side effect. After two years of nothing but constipation, she was looking forward to getting some diarrhea for once. We told the doctor about her last cycle having been exceptionally brutal during the first 4 days of the cycle (EX-

TREME fatigue, constipation, unable to eat, and was down to just 130 pounds). The doctor said that, after two years into chemo, the cumulative effect was now a very real thing. Andrea kept forcing herself to do chemo even though she knew how miserable it made her. "But," she said, "if it gives me even one more day with you and my daughter, then it's worth it." We'd already had a couple of conversations with the doctor about when to quit chemo. Up to that point, Andrea was able to gain back weight and be somewhat functional toward the end of cycles, but everything we did (or didn't do) entirely revolved around what point of the cycle she was in. We almost had it down to a science until Irinotecan/Camptosar was added, and then we had to re-learn how to cope.

Fortunately, the universe gifted Andrea a coping buddy. Our friends Kale and Gabby asked us to babysit their kitties while they were in Washington state for a couple weeks – one of which they'd rescued from being euthanized right before they'd left North Dakota. During those two weeks, sitting by the fire together, Andrea fell in love with the kitty whom Kale had named "Squirrel" because of the way she sat up. Indeed, Squirrel looked like her namesake while sitting. It was the best way for her to see her surroundings, given her disability, with her little T-rex arms. Squirrel was born with radial hypoplasia, a genetic mutation that causes a deformity of the radius bone. Veterinarians sometimes call them "squitten" cats (squirrel + kitten = squitten). They're often smaller than normal, like the runt of the litter. We started calling her "Baby Squirrel Kitten," or BSK for short. While Squirrel wasn't technically up for adoption, Andrea asked Gabby if we could adopt her. Andrea offered $500 as an adoption fee, but Gabby said we could adopt without paying an adoption fee because she knew we would take good care of Squirrel. We understood her joint deformity meant she limped when walking, that her joints would get arthritic as she aged, and that she would always be small. At the time we adopted her, Squirrel was 3 years old and only 4.5 pounds. Being underweight was the reason she hadn't been spayed in North Dakota (and it was cheaper to euthanize rather than spay/neuter, especially for animals deemed "unadoptable"). The day after we officially adopted Squirrel, I noticed an unusual discharge coming from her hind end. I collected a sample and took her to the vet. She was immediately diagnosed with Pyometra using the sample I provided, then rushed into emergency surgery to save her life. The surgery cost $1,500, but we saved her life – and Andrea got to tell Gabby, "See! I told you we'd pay to adopt Squirrel!" That was the second time Squirrel was rescued from certain death (that we know of). Squirrel repaid us with love, snuggles, cuddles, companionship, and later became Andrea's hospice support kitty – and then my grief support kitty.

Soon after Squirrel recovered from surgery, more additions to our household arrived. My daughter and her three kitties came from New York to live with us. Moving in with your mother and her dying partner during a worldwide pandemic probably isn't something that most 21-year-olds would do. I tried to explain to my daughter how things would only get worse with cancer, but neither of us really understood just how bad it would get. About a week after her arrival in Alaska, I was driving my daughter to her first shift working at the mall when she received a call from her store manager that the entire building was shutting down due to the pandemic.

For Andrea, COVID-19 was now an added concern on top of cancer. Due to the risks to her immune system, Andrea's oncologist recommended deferring her chemo treatment – again. With so many uncertainties about the virus, it wasn't a good time to do anything that weakened anyone's immune systems. For Andrea, after two years of chemo, being immune compromised meant being at higher risk for just about everything; and since my daughter had just traveled from NY, it was too risky for Andrea to do chemo. The Cancer Center was being extra cautious and testing anyone with symptoms (including household members), deferring treatments, and limiting who could enter the hospital. The first confirmed COVID-19 case in Fairbanks happened the same day Andrea was supposed be at that hospital for chemo. We decided it was time we hunkered down. Thankfully, our friends, again, saved our butts by helping us out with food and supplies. Without their generosity, we would not have been prepared. We were so fortunate to have a community of friends who made such a difference.

Isolation quickly got old. Andrea missed people coming over to visit, especially her daughter. We'd been trying to navigate how cancer and chemo worked during a pandemic. The doctors and nurses didn't really know either. They told us they were literally making it up as they went, doing their best to adjust as things changed. They understood the seriousness of the situation and were doing everything possible to reduce the risks to patients and staff. Everyone was getting tested, but sometimes it took 2 weeks to get the results back (as it did in our case). Even so, the oncologist said Andrea could continue chemo treatments, but that we needed to be flexible if things changed. Her next infusion wouldn't be "business as usual;" they were not allowing anyone in the building except the patient – so I couldn't go – and EVERYONE was required to wear PPE the entire time. We also had to get clearance from a PA to use Andrea's chemo port because it developed an infected-looking stitch on one side. Our other concern was the possibility that we may be forced to cancel or reschedule Andrea's Celebration of Life (that we'd booked for June 27). At least we weren't worried about Andrea's brain aneurysm because the MRI the previous month showed it was "stable" and unchanged. So, we just focused on staying home and restarting her chemo treatments (and being willing to adjust as things changed). In the month that she'd been off chemo, she'd experienced more painful effects from the cancer growth, so she wanted to get back on treatment to control it.

April 2020 turned out to be Andrea's last birthday. At the time, I didn't want to accept that possibility. Between the early days of the pandemic and all the Trump shenanigans in the news, there were enough distractions to keep my mind from wandering too far from the day-to-day focus of caregiving. Andrea's mother gave her a custom homemade quilt for her birthday that had purple patterns on one side and cats on the other. Four months later, we used that quilt as part of our wedding (purple is our favorite color).

Soon after her birthday, Andrea hit a breaking point with her pain levels. We called the doctor and explained her symptoms and our concerns; he immediately ordered a CT scan. The results showed significant disease progression as indicated by fluid and distension around the bowel and more obstruction causing extreme pain when stool passed by the tumors in the colon and rectum. Her oncologist consulted with the specialist in Seattle about how to best modify her chemo regimen, but the new plan required the doctor to fight with insurance to get it approved; the regular course of action wasn't appropriate because of the risks of surgery, so it took time to get the right chemo drugs sufficiently justified for insurance to pay. As is often the case, treatment comes down to fighting with insurance. The effort required of providers and patients to effectively battle insurance has got to be one of the biggest wastes of time – for those who have the least of it. Nobody should have to fight cancer AND the system at the same time. The insurance ultimately denied the oncologist's request to change Andrea's chemo regimen, so we reverted back to the previous regimen until the doctor felt like fighting the insurance again.

This is about the time we realized Andrea wouldn't be able to have her Celebration of Life as we'd originally planned. She had wanted a big party with an open bar, with everyone wearing their favorite band T-shirts. We'd reserved a venue for June 27, 2020, which was too early in the pandemic for large gatherings. It broke my heart that the world couldn't stop for one evening so we could celebrate her life. Many, including myself, offered Andrea various alternative celebration ideas that we could do instead. I asked Andrea what alternatives she preferred, while making it clear that I only wanted whatever she wanted. She said "no" to everything. She insisted that since she couldn't do it the way she'd planned, then she didn't want to do it at all. Although it made me very sad, I respected her decision. I always supported Andrea's choices for her life, even if it wasn't what I would have chosen. True love means accepting, respecting and supporting our loved one's decisions, even when we would prefer something else. So, we canceled all the plans for her Celebration of Life. Andrea's Go Fund Me page was changed to indicate that all donations would instead be going toward her cremation costs.

By mid-June, we were forced to cancel all of Andrea's medical appointments. She was abruptly dropped by Medicaid insurance and there was no way possible for us to pay for her treatment out-of-pocket. We called numerous times and each person we spoke with was either unwilling or unable to reinstate her coverage. Chemo had been holding back her tumors, but without coverage, it felt like an instant death sentence. The billing department at the Cancer Center contacted a hospital worker who specialized in Alaska State Medicaid to see if they could assist. They claimed Andrea no longer qualified under Expansion Medicaid nor Disabled Medicaid. They indicated that the State had changed their qualification rules, which meant Andrea's Social Security disability benefits put her over the income threshold. Our next move was to contact Alaska's elected officials in Washington, D.C., going above Governor Dunleavy who obviously didn't care about people on Medicaid (he'd cut the funding). I spent hours on the phone with various agencies and experts trying to understand what happened, what we could do, and what resources were available for people in Andrea's situation. The Aging and Disability Resources Center talked with me extensively about the details of Andrea's case. We were advised to call Alaska Legal Services to set up something called a Miller Trust that makes Social Security and other disability income exempt from calculations of income if the State is reimbursed from the trust for Medicaid expenses upon the recipient's death. In order for Andrea to continue cancer treatment, she needed to re-qualify for Medicaid, but first, part of her disability benefits must be put into a trust (that Medicaid would eventually get). This was another lesson in how the system is frustratingly convoluted. Trying to navigate all that was ridiculous. Until then, I didn't know disabled people needed a lawyer to set up a trust to take their benefits so they could get healthcare. I made sure to explain to every person I talked with about how awful this was – and THEY ALL AGREED.

We started a letter writing campaign. Andrea's friends wrote to elected officials to make the case for changes to the system. Following is the letter I sent:

The U.S. healthcare system is so convoluted and difficult to navigate. So many different insurance plans, with no consistency in what's covered and what's not, eligibility requirements, various premiums/deductibles/co-pays, denials, appeals, pre-approvals, pre-existing conditions, exemptions, and terminations. It's a hot mess. The whole thing makes it nearly impossible for an elderly or disabled person to navigate, let alone an average citizen. Full disclosure: I'm a relatively privileged, educated white woman. But

I've been flabbergasted by the hoops I've had to jump through, the red tape, the bureaucracy that I've been forced to wade through as a caregiver and patient advocate for my terminally ill partner. I could literally write a book. What about the rest of us? What about people of color, less privilege, less education? How are they to navigate this system? No wonder so many people fall through the cracks. No wonder so many just give up and die. Most of us simply don't have the energy it takes to fight the system while sick. This system is oppressive, exclusionary, and contributes to structural violence. The richest country in the world has the highest number of bankruptcies due to medical debt. The system values profits over people. Only the rich, or those who have the best insurance, can access this system. The rest of us are left to piecemeal our needs together by applying to this program or that program, this agency or that agency. It's time to end this mess. We need universal healthcare. We need a simple system that deems you worthy of quality healthcare by virtue of being a human being. Period. No more care based on wealth or association or lack thereof. No more piecemeal. We need to make healthcare a human right in this country. Anything less is inhumane.

Finally, we got a call from Medicaid. They said they were able to use the newly announced coronavirus policy to temporarily reinstate Andrea's coverage. Because of COVID-19, they were allowed to approve Medicaid coverage for anyone who needed it – without considering income eligibility requirements. Although temporary, this was still a huge relief. We were informed that we'd still need to set up the Miller Trust, but at least now we'd have time to do it. I literally sobbed when they told us. How ironic that it took a worldwide pandemic to save us in that moment. They said we had until the end of the year to get the trust set up, so I called the Disability Law Center to see if they could do the required paperwork (because Alaska Legal Services denied us). And, with Andrea's insurance reinstated, I called the Cancer Center and got all her treatment appointments rescheduled. I was exhausted. Despite seeking help, suggestions and moral support as we'd navigated the system, it was still a rollercoaster. The representative at the Disability Resource Center said, "You should sell your story to Lifetime for one of those made-for-TV-movies and make millions – then at least you'd have a legitimate reason to get kicked off Medicaid."

The daily realities of Stage IV colorectal cancer were less than pleasant. With abdominal pain, discomfort, distention, cramping, tightness/hardness and lack of bowel movements, it was possible Andrea had an intestinal blockage or restriction. An abdominal ultrasound didn't show anything except stool in the way. Despite all the stool softeners, laxatives, suppositories and enemas, Andrea was only able to produce what she called "rabbit poops." She decided to defer her chemo appointment again. If things didn't improve, the doctor would likely order an emergency CT scan hoping to see something (although they couldn't see much on her previous CT because there was too much fluid in the way). Our RN friend told us, "I'm shocked at all the CTs they keep doing. Isn't that adding more fuel to the cancer fire? An MRI is safer and more detailed – but takes longer and costs more." I knew it was unlikely that Medicaid would pay for an MRI. And when Andrea attempted to request an MRI, it only resulted in an argument with the radiologist. As if it wasn't already frustrating and irritating for Andrea battling what she called "bathroom issues" every day for 3 years, her pain only increased over the summer and significantly reduced her ability to function – but she still refused to take pain medications. She repeatedly said, "I don't want to be Fairbanks' next heroin addict."

Finally, after a month of debilitating pain and CT results showing ascites (excess fluid in the abdomen), they finally got Andrea in for a paracentesis (a procedure to remove fluid). The delay was due to a COVID-19 policy that only allowed for life-saving procedures, so we had to wait for the ban on all other procedures to be lifted. However, they ended up not doing the procedure because the stenographer and doctor agreed that there wasn't enough fluid to make it worth doing. It is rare for ascites to reduce without intervention, so everyone was confused about how that happened. Despite the non-procedure, it was worth the trip to the hospital because we FINALLY got to have a REAL conversation with the new PA at the Cancer Center. It was the first time anyone there had been honest with us, validated our concerns and questions, and NOT tried to sugarcoat everything. He even used words like "terminal" and "DNR." We talked about Andrea's abdominal pain, extreme fatigue, sleeping 20 hours a day, unable to get out of bed, lack of appetite, constipation, and how there were no breaks between cycles anymore (she had these symptoms even when she was off chemo). After we talked, we all agreed that hospice was the right avenue to pursue. He put in the consultation, and two hours later hospice called to schedule an in-home consultation. We were unsure how to feel. Anxious and relieved all at the same time? It was a scary step forward, but it helped knowing that experienced people who had been there before would be helping guide the way. Still, I was so overwhelmed that I only remember two things from that first meeting with hospice: the nurses explained they weren't allowed to "delay nor facilitate death," and Andrea proudly told them she would be "the best die-er ever." Even in the most serious moments, Andrea found a way to make us laugh.

By mid-July, Andrea's symptoms/problems grew (too many to list), and she suspected that she didn't have much time left. After a consultation with her doctor, we found out that Andrea was right: she was starving. Her urine test confirmed it. We canceled all her chemo appointments, and she officially began hospice care (her doctor agreed she was within the 6-month window). Honestly, I looked forward to hospice support so that I could hopefully avoid caregiver burnout. Unfortunately, because of COVID-19, supports and programs for caregivers had been suspended. Hospice volunteers and respite providers weren't allowed into patient's homes; only staff with proper PPE were authorized.

Andrea began telling me things as if she would be dying soon, requesting things she wanted me to keep (or not), things to give or tell other people, thanking me for taking care of her and loving her, and repeatedly insisting I try to be happy and enjoy my life. We shared a lot of tears. Everyone provided kind words and offered to help, but I was so overwhelmed that it was impossible for me to respond to everyone individually – and my brain was doing a terrible job of thinking of things that others could help with, especially given the COVID-19 restrictions. So, I tried to answer some of the questions people had by making the following Q&A post on her private Facebook page:

Q - Can Andrea visit via phone or video chat? A - Right now, she's just so weak that even speaking requires too much energy. I've told her names of people who have offered to talk (or you may have messaged her directly) and she will try to call you if/when she's feeling up to it.

Q - Because she's had so many bowel issues, can't they just give her a colostomy bag? A - No, the colostomy bag is not an option. The doctor said it's way too risky a procedure for someone like Andrea and would be way outside of "standard of care," meaning insurance would never cover it.

Q - What were the results of her paracentesis? A - We're still waiting for the call to schedule the next paracentesis.

Q - Are there any cancer treatments left for her to try? A - Andrea's doctor said there's a "last resort" chemo drug that typically gives patients about 2 months of life, but it has some pretty horrible side effects. If a patient is already weak (like Andrea) then they generally don't suggest it.

Q - Is there a way to send financial assistance toward her final expenses? A - Yes, Andrea has a GoFundMe.

Andrea's 2nd paracentesis procedure was unsuccessful, for the same reason as before: not enough fluid to make it worth doing. That meant the pain/bloating/distention was caused by something else besides fluid – most likely cancer growth. The oncologist said hospice was completely appropriate but that he also wanted to see if there was anything else he could come up with for her to try; however, he said, most of the options left at that point wouldn't be covered by insurance. In the meantime, Andrea was literally starving. I'd been tracking her caloric intake for weeks and she was definitely not taking in enough to survive much longer. The doctor confirmed she was experiencing cachexia (characterized by weight loss, low appetite, loss of muscle mass, malabsorption, and extreme fatigue). Most late-stage cancer patients die of cachexia (essentially starving to death). Once cachexia begins, it's almost impossible to reverse. Because her time was so short, I asked if she still wanted to get married and she said "yes." A hospital notary graciously came to our house to notarize our marriage license application for a deathbed wedding. While we waited for the application to be processed, I started making arrangements and everyone was eager to contribute something to make it the best wedding possible under the circumstances.

During the first week of hospice care, we had nearly daily visits (nurses, home health aides, medical social worker, Chaplin) and medical equipment delivered from the hospital – all while planning our wedding! Thankfully, the hospice nurses were finally successful in convincing Andrea to try medications to control pain, so she was better able to participate and express her wishes. Several friends were instrumental in helping, arranging, and donating everything from food to flowers. By mid-2020, everyone was attending events online, so we invited friends/family near and far to join us for our non-traditional/COVID/Zoom/deathbed wedding ceremony. Squirrel decided to be the cat-of-honor and made herself the center of attention, lying next to Andrea the entire time. Clearly, it was really Squirrel's wedding, and she merely allowed us to attend. At one point, I jokingly asked Andrea, "Are you marrying me, or the cat?"

On August 2, 2020, in the most beautiful way, Reverend Leslie Ahuvah Fails of United Universalist Fellowship of Fairbanks officiated our ceremony using the following script:

> Let us take a moment to center ourselves, to bring ourselves fully into the sacred space of this moment.
> Hear these words from Margaret Keip —
> As surely as we belong to the universe
> we belong together.
> We join here to transcend the isolated self,
> to reconnect,
> to know ourselves to be at home,
> here on earth, under the stars,
> linked with each other.
> WELCOME FRIENDS AND FAMILY
> As the poet James Kavanaugh wrote —
> To love is not to possess,
> To own or imprison,
> Nor to lose one's self in another.
> Love is to join and separate,
> To walk alone and together,
> To find a laughing freedom

That lonely isolation does not permit.
It is finally to be able
To be who we really are
No longer clinging in childish dependency
Nor docilely living separate lives in silence,
It is to be perfectly one's self
And perfectly joined in permanent commitment
To another--and to one's inner self.
Love only endures when it moves like waves,
Receding and returning gently or passionately,
Or moving lovingly like the tide
In the moon's own predictable harmony,
Because finally, despite a child's scars
Or an adult's deepest wounds,
They are openly free to be
Who they really are--and always secretly were,
In the very core of their being
Where true and lasting love can alone abide.

As individuals, Andrea and Melanie, you are each the result of the love of thousands. In this moment, surrounded by
the love of your community, you are also in the presence of
countless ancestors. You have each been on your own journey, and you have known joy and grief and happiness and
sorrow, both separately and together. On your own, each of
you are complete human beings, each with your own lives,
your own hopes and dreams.

You have already loved, supported, and cared for one another through trials and disappointments, through grief and
joy. Your relationship has been a source of comfort and joy,
both for you and for your adult children — and a place of
shelter for renewal and rest. Today we make true in the eyes
of the state that which has already been true for a long time

— and perhaps, since long before you met — that the two of you are one heart.

Today we honor the miracle of your becoming. We honor the roller coaster of love and loss that you have each been on, separately and together, throughout your lives. We celebrate the miracle that you found one another in the first place, and that — against all odds — you were reunited after being separated early in your relationship. We celebrate that, against all odds, you kindled in one another a bravery that allowed you to emerge from struggle and pain to become the women that you are now. We give thanks for the home that you have created together, for the sanctuary of safety and love that you have built.

I hold science as one of my dearest spiritual teachers. Thousands of years of observation by scientists and philosophers has taught us that the universe, the world we live in, is full of energy — the electric energy of lightning bolts, of static that pops when we wear a sweater in cold weather, the flickering luminescence of fireflies, the mechanical energy of a wild river in motion ... the numinous spark between human beings in love.

But while this energy frequently changes from one form to another, it never disappears. A stick of dynamite explodes, converting chemical energy into kinetic energy. The law of Conservation of Energy assures us that "Energy cannot be created or destroyed." In other words, the total amount of energy in the universe never changes, although it may change from one form to another. Energy never disappears, but it does change form.

I have no reason to believe that the electricity that causes our hearts to beat is somehow exempt from the same physical laws that govern the electricity of lightning bolts and fireflies. Melanie explained to me that the universe has had a habit of separating the two of you in messed up ways, and also of reuniting you in ways that have bordered on the miraculous. Whatever lies ahead for you, my dear Andrea and Melanie, I know this much is true — the two of you will remain united in love.

The same love that has carried you through separation and distance before stands ready to carry you, to carry all of us, come what may.

Andrea and Melanie, we give thanks for you. We give thanks for the miracle of your relationship. We give thanks for all that you are. We give thanks for all you have made possible by your love for one another. You are a blessing to each other, and to each of us.

> Begin unity candle ritual
> VOWS / RING EXCHANGE
> This ring is an endless circle
> And it holds my promise to you
> My heart is your shelter
> And my arms are your home
> With this ring I give you all that I am
> And all that I will become.
> BLESSINGS from friends and family on Zoom: Offer a one-word blessing for Melanie and Andrea. As the music plays, please type your blessings into the chat box.
> Pronouncement and kiss.

As beautiful as it was, our wedding was bittersweet. I remember it both fondly and painfully. Worst of all, it wasn't the wedding that Andrea deserved. Covid and cancer made it a deathbed wedding. I did the best I could (as did others), but nobody could fix the world and give her the day she deserved. For me, that still "stings." The reasons we couldn't get married sooner just added salt to the wounds. Firstly, if we were legally married, the house would've become marital property, and the IRS would take it to pay back a lien. Secondly, Andrea would lose part of her disability benefits because my income would count against her. Thirdly, I wouldn't have been allowed to be her PCA/DSP with Access Alaska because Medicaid doesn't allow spouses to be caregivers. Those were 3 very negative impacts. So, unless Andrea wanted to be homeless, with reduced income and substandard care, she couldn't get married until death was imminent.

Incidentally, the IRS lien wasn't her fault. A former employer from 20 years prior had failed to report to the IRS. Every employee was affected, not just Andrea. When the IRS finally caught up to them, the company had already ceased to exist. But the IRS made all employees of the dead company pay back taxes anyway. They claimed Andrea owed them $60,000. Her lien and my divorce were the reasons we couldn't get a loan from ANYONE to build our house. Every bank and credit union denied us. So, we built it on our own, doing all the labor ourselves, paycheck by paycheck, over 5 years. Because of cancer, the house never got finished, but at least we weren't homeless. On her deathbed, Andrea apologized to me for not finishing the house. It was our one big dream, but that dream died unfinished – just like our lives together. After a lot of heartache and headache, I sold the house "as is" a few years later.

CHAPTER 7: WHOSE PAIN IS IT, ANYWAY?

We had a difficult time following the wedding. It was a challenging adjustment going from FIGHTING CANCER to "preparing for death." Neither of us wanted to give up. There was a great deal of grief processing that happened in that transition. I later learned I'd already been experiencing something called "anticipatory grief." I couldn't fully accept the reality of our situation; it's like my brain couldn't process it. I didn't want to believe that the universe had brought us together, only to rip us apart. It just felt too unfair – too much of an injustice – to be true. In my mind, I thought our love for each other could somehow overcome the horrors of a slow death by cancer. If anyone deserved a miracle, surely, it was Andrea. My brain couldn't accept otherwise.

Hospice staff were wonderful, but it took a great deal of trial-and-error to figure out the right combination of medications, doses, and frequency to find a "happy medium" between extreme pain and extreme drowsiness. Managing medications became my primary task. I set multiple alarms on my phone to keep track of them all (I still have those alarm settings in my phone because, for some reason, I can't bear to delete them). This gave me a false sense of control, as if administering her medications perfectly would somehow save her. It wasn't until months later that I had to accept the bitter reality that despite my very best caregiving, I couldn't cure cancer. I hated that fact. I resisted it. Undeterred, I poured myself into caregiving around the clock. I simply couldn't live with myself unless I could say I'd done everything I could possibly do. And I hoped that somehow my love and my diligence in following medical protocol would translate into a miracle.

We learned that hospice care was not universal. Although it was supposed to be paid for by federal Medicare funds, it depended on location. Some places had no hospice options at all. Other places had a full range of hospice services, from in-home care to dedicated facilities. Some offered a variety of services for family members, both before and after the patient's death. In Alaska, only larger communities had dedicated hospice programs. Smaller communities had to choose between dying in a hospital hundreds of miles away from loved ones, or staying in their communities and dying without hospice supports. All patients had to leave the state if they wanted to choose legal Death With Dignity options. Nearly all options were limited nationwide during 2020 due to COVID-19. At the time, we did not realize how the limitations would impact us. Later, we learned that Andrea's only option was in-home care (which she preferred) because there was no dedicated facility in Fairbanks at the time. And her original plan to pursue Death With Dignity in Washington state became impossible due to their overwhelmed healthcare system and Andrea's inability to travel. This fact was probably the most devastating blow to Andrea's morale. She felt it was inhumane that she was deprived of choices for her own life and death. She made her wishes known to anyone who would listen, especially hospice staff who understandably lamented their lack of options. Hospice staff were already limited by the amount of time they could spend in a patient's home and by the laws preventing them from facilitating death; then, they were further limited by COVID-19 restrictions. It was a terrible predicament for everyone involved.

Andrea was in bed 99% of the time. Between the effects of the cancer, cachexia, and the medications, extreme fatigue was her primary issue. But at least we'd finally learned how to better manage her pain levels. She was on a liquid diet, but still had significant problems with bowel movements and rectal prolapse. The tumor burden in her abdomen was wreaking havoc on everything from her diaphragm (triggering hiccups) to her rectum (triggering painful muscle spasms). With her entire abdomen full of tumors, EVERYTHING was painful. Cough, sneeze, laugh or hiccup, and she'd be doubled over in excruciating pain. There was no way to fix it. We could only mask it. For 3 years, Andrea fought against taking pain meds, but now she had no choice. By far, the worst pain was in the bathroom. Hospice had prescribed meds for muscle spasms, which was the only thing that kept her off super high doses of pain meds. But we learned so much the hard way! By that point, we'd had two significant crisis situations when her pain/anxiety were completely out of control, where I had to call hospice late at night to get instructions on what to do. Once the pain/anxiety was out of control, it was extremely difficult to get back on top of it. Both times required liquid sublingual Morphine, which was the only non-IV pain management that was somewhat effective for her. During the worst episode, Andrea's rectum prolapsed 8-9 times during a 30-minute period. She was begging me to shoot her, saying she was "done with this shit," asking me where I'd hid the gun, asking why the State of Alaska doesn't have Death With Dignity, asking why she can't end her suffering when SHE decided to. Later, when we discussed this with the hospice nurses, they agreed and said they wished that option was available. They also confirmed there had been cases in Fairbanks where desperate hospice patients "took matters into their own hands."

Many well-meaning people asked what they could do to help, and I wished I knew what to tell them. Aside from changing laws or having a cure for cancer, there was no way to fix our situation. No matter what we did, it was going to suck. The question was more about the DEGREE of "suckiness." Friends who offered food, funds, and errand-running helped make things suck less. In a non-COVID world, it would have been different because we'd have had plenty of friends, family, and hospice volunteers coming all the time. But because we lived in a COVID world, none of that support was recommended. The best we could do was to request that people drop things on the doorstep and wave from the window. But what I REALLY wanted was to eat together, cry together, and hug each other. Also, I lost my job (with Access Alaska) as Andrea's PCA/DSP as soon as we were legally married. I continued to do the work, but I was not getting paid for it anymore. This put more strain on our finances and caused more worry during an already worrisome situation. Once again, friends came to the rescue with what Rev. Lesile called "the casserole brigade" to help with meals. At a time when many felt helpless, meals provided a tangible way for people to do something to show they cared about us. Most of the time I'd just get a text message saying "I put something on your doorstep! Love you both!" and we'd cry while waving to one another from the front window.

During this time, Dr. Sine Anahita, a UAF sociologist and artist, was working on a project about death and grief. She asked Andrea if she would be interested in being a model for this project, and Andrea agreed. So, Sine came to our home several times to observe and take photos to use as reference. Sine also promised that Andrea would have final approval over her works of art. Below are the first two pieces Sine completed, along with their titles and her description of each.

ANDREA

Anahita

She is Being Swept Away

Andrea struggled for three years against colon cancer. Near the end, I asked her if I could chronicle her journey. She graciously said yes. In this drawing, I imagine that she was being swept away from us by a raging river or some other force over which none of us have any control.

The Harbinger

Owls have long been associated with being harbingers of one kind or another. They are often the harbinger of Death. Owls are also celebrated as bringers of Wisdom, and of being spirit animals. I imagined that this Great Grey Owl perched next to her as a symbol that Death was approaching.

As the cancer took over more and more, Andrea continued to lose weight. Her muscles atrophied. She had little appetite and most food was repulsive to her. But, because most of her medications had to be given with food, our compromise was Ensure shakes. The vanilla flavor was the only one she could tolerate. So, I started buying them by the case at Costco. Squirrel started to learn that my phone alarms went off every 6 to 8 hours to remind me to administer Andrea's medications, along with an Ensure shake. Squirrel would follow me and supervise Andrea as she took her medications each time. Andrea would pour a small amount of Ensure into the bottle cap and allowed Squirrel to lick it. Both underweight, Andrea was starving while Squirrel was gaining. Squirrel came to expect her little "milkshakes" that Andrea gave her. When each alarm would sound, Squirrel would come running! The difference was that Squirrel's body was able to absorb the nutrients, but Andrea's body was unable to absorb much of anything because cancer had essentially taken over her GI tract. All my diligent efforts to administer her meds on time, around the clock, and months of constantly offering food and water – turned out to be futile. Very little of it could be absorbed by her intestines. She was doomed to starve to death. She described to me what it felt like to be starving – like her body was eating itself from the inside out. Oral pain medication (liquid morphine) to manage her symptoms was only marginally effective, as sublingual was her only absorption route.

At the beginning of September, Andrea strained so hard in the bathroom that she broke a blood vessel in her eye. This was just a small manifestation of the bowel pain she endured daily. Pain management was continually a work in progress. Hospice nurses finally convinced her that her pain would get worse, not better. She agreed to try a Fentanyl patch, which she'd resisted for a long time. The nurses said Fentanyl was more consistent in the body as opposed to Norco that rollercoasters every 6 hours. However, Andrea barely made it a day with the Fentanyl patch because she had an allergic reaction to it. She had 2 symptoms under "seek emergency medical assistance" listed in the info paper that comes with the patch. I called Hospice and they told me to remove the patch immediately and give her Benadryl. We went back to the Norco regimen and supplemented with oral liquid Morphine.

Andrea's final wish was to live to see Trump out of office. Election Day was the first week of November and it was unclear whether she would live to see fulfillment of that wish, especially since results were expected to be contested either way. Politics under Trump was painful, but even more so when your humanity was denied. Andrea had her own opinions about the hateful rhetoric Trump spewed about transgender people, racial minorities, and disabled people – because she was all three. She asked me to please ensure she received a mail-in ballot so she could vote before she died. She wanted to do her part to be a voice for other people like her.

Andrea also continued to share her thoughts regarding Death With Dignity. "I'm upset that I don't get the choice because of somebody else's religious beliefs; we need legislation without religion involved" she said. When the hospice Chaplin called me to check in, I gave him all the updates. When I got to the part about Andrea wishing she had Death With Dignity options, he said he'd heard of hospice nurses telling patients to "just stop eating and drinking." In the moment, I was shocked by this but didn't say anything. After I told Andrea, she became angry and said that was "the stupidest advice." She explained it this way: "If a dog was dying of cancer, would you starve it to death? No! You'd do the humane thing! Why can't I get the same respect as a dog?"

How could I argue with that? She was right. If she was a dog, she would have better options for a humane death. And yes, she deserved the same dignity as a dog! It broke my heart that I couldn't provide what she rightfully deserved. The amount of pain she was in had to be inhumane by anyone's standards. And it was universally agreed that she would not beat cancer; it would kill her. She was very aware and mentally keen about everything. Unlike most patients who experience cognitive decline due to cancer spreading to their brain, Andrea's cancer never went beyond her abdomen. So, unfortunately, she was all too aware of her suffering and her lack of choice in the matter. We asked about an epidural, but we were told they couldn't do it in the home setting – nor any IV pain management. Andrea would have to be hospitalized, and she refused go there because it was overrun with COVID-19 and I wouldn't be allowed to be with her. So, her symptoms worsened, especially her abdominal distention. If you've ever seen the belly of someone who is 7-8 months pregnant, that's what it looked like. Even the new hospice doctor was surprised by Andrea's noticeably distended abdomen. After examining her, the doctor confirmed the distention was due to rapid cancer growth (tumors). Unfortunately, he said, it would only get worse. Eventually the cancer growth would prevent Andrea from being able to eat, drink, or pass stool – resulting in death. All we could do was continue subpar pain management for her.

As usual, with Andrea's permission, I made periodic posts on her private Facebook group with updates about her struggle. With so many people at home during the first year of the pandemic, we received a lot of reactions and comments on these posts. Below is a small sampling of them.

- Amy: "My heart shatters for you both, her from the pain and suffering. It shatters for you because to watch your soulmate in pain and suffering while you yourself are also suffering and trying to wrap your head around all of this and usually doing it alone since no one can come help you. I wish I had the words to take away your pain. I wish I had the cure to take away her pain and cure her. I feel helpless but know I'm there. I see you. I hear you."
- Heather: "I wish death with dignity was nationwide... it should be."
- Sarah: "I don't ever have any words when I read these posts. I just always have this heavy heart, and a lot of feelings. I'm genuinely so sorry that you're both having to endure this. If I could hug you, help you, or just be near you, I would. Seriously sending you both so much love."
- Areta: "I wish there was a better way for Andrea to get over her situation with dignity and by her willing. I'm not for end-of-life methods but I do agree that there are situations that are so hard to survive that they should at least take care properly to it. Andrea is one of those cases and I think she already fought enough and suffered enough in these years that she should have the right to decide."

In mid-September, our friends from Anchorage came to see Andrea. They gifted me a custom-made necklace with flanking purple pearls and a center plate that read "f*ck cancer." I loved it so much and wore it continuously (Andrea requested that, after her death, I place our wedding rings on either side of the necklace to symbolize that we were separated by cancer). They also brought their cute doggie and hung out with Andrea while she drank her favorite pink wine and enjoyed each other's company and conversation. These friends were an invaluable source of support and love throughout our journey.

Andrea's stomach continued to be pressured by all the abdominal tumors, which caused lots of problems: acid reflux, heartburn, nausea, vomiting, and inability to eat or drink. Experiencing cachexia, Andrea was like most cancer patients, essentially starving to death. She was down to 129 pounds, had lost nearly all muscle tone, and her face was starting to sink in. We knew her time was short, so she was having little visits with close friends and family. One of them asked her for any words of advice that she could pass on. Here is how she answered:

1. If you get diagnosed with Stage IV Cancer, don't do chemo. Just live your best life until you can't. The misery of chemo just isn't worth it.

2. Be true to yourself, be who you are, and be happy! Life is too short to be miserable.

3. Don't work at Bassett. (Bassett was the name of the Army hospital she worked at for 13 years, on-call 24/7 with no vacations, endured anti-trans harassment and discrimination until terminated, and where she was potentially exposed to radiation).

Andrea repeatedly expressed the desire to NOT starve to death, to NOT let cancer take her, that she wanted to go on HER terms. Her symptoms worsened and she made the decision that September 27 would be her last day. She asked important family/friends to be present and requested that they support her and respect her decision. She spent the two days prior calling loved ones far and near to say goodbye, sent farewell messages on text and Messenger, and allowed a few to say goodbye in person. She had received information from several different medical professionals, and she was confident that she had enough medication.

When the day came, she met with key people that she'd invited to be present. Many tears were shed by all. We used nearly an entire Costco case of Kleenex that day! It was incredibly emotional and powerful to see how much love we all had for her! Both of her parents sat in our living room while Andrea explained, again, her reasons and asked that they respect her decision. Her father was also dying and probably should've been on hospice care at the same time as Andrea, so he said he understood. Her mother seemed reluctant and frustrated by the situation that her child was in. Our wonderful Death Doula sat with Andrea's mother and the other guests. After she said her goodbyes, Andrea retreated to her bedroom with just a few witnesses to enjoy her last moments. She did all the things that she hadn't been able to do in months: eat solid food, smoke cannabis, and drink wine. Then, when she was ready, she swallowed all the liquid morphine. She said it was the hardest thing she had ever done.

Then, we waited. The medical information we'd been told indicated the process would be relatively quick – just a matter of minutes. But in Andrea's case, that was not what happened. Everyone had failed to take into account that the cancer has severely impacted the ability of her GI tract to absorb anything, so her system was extremely slow in processing the morphine. She intentionally took 3 times the lethal dose because, she said, "I don't want to wake up." Instead, what happened was she never went to sleep! She partied all night, talking to friends and family, telling jokes and stories, playing guitar – all very entertaining! She ended up having a Celebration of Life!

We didn't have a back-up plan, nor permission from Andrea about what to do, in the event that her attempt failed. She was understandably frustrated and upset that her original plan didn't work the way she had intended, but at least she had a great time with those who loved her. And she did ALL THE THINGS! I hadn't seen her that happy in 3 years! However, all the solid food came back up when she vomited 10 hours later. But if you party like a Rock Star, you'll have a hangover, right? And, my goodness, she was the talk of the town when the medical professionals learned that she was awake all night partying after ingesting 3 times the lethal amount! They were flabbergasted! None of them had ever had a patient survive swallowing that much morphine. They said Andrea was a medical marvel!

Technically, the cannabis and alcohol should have intensified the effect of the morphine. But because Andrea's GI track had a severely depressed absorption rate (due to cancer), everything was processed at a snail's pace. That was why she could ride the high for so long. For a few hours overnight she had depressed respiration and elevated pulse, but not enough to be lethal. We found out 2 days later that she definitely had an intestinal blockage that was preventing almost everything from moving from the stomach to the small intestine. That's why she vomited everything. Only small amounts of water were barely seeping through. She was not passing stool anymore, just water. At that rate, she wouldn't be able to last much longer. Unfortunately, she felt defeated about not being able to end it on her own terms.

A hospice nurse said to me, "I think you should champion a Death With Dignity act for Alaska and call it Andrea's Law." I couldn't have agreed more. I think anyone with a terminal illness should have the option to end their suffering on their own terms and have medical staff on-hand to ensure the patient's desires are fulfilled. If Andrea had that option in Alaska, she would've had her wishes honored. But instead, she had to take matters into her own hands and risk having a different outcome than desired. As much as I wanted to change the laws, I knew it had already been tried several times in Alaska, and it never made it past the state legislature. Also, Andrea had been consistently insistent that I leave the country as soon as possible. "I don't want you, or someone you love in the future, to experience this again," she told me.

While we were all glad to have more time with Andrea, it came with a level of sadness because she was still suffering. We were glad she got to have an unexpected Celebration of Life party, but sad that her final wish failed. The whole experience was an intense emotional rollercoaster, which nobody wanted to do again. Thankfully, everyone allowed us to be intimate, vulnerable, authentic and open about our experience. Generally, these topics are taboo to talk about, so people don't realize how often this happens and how hard it is. We hoped our experiences helped to open conversations – as society needs to be better at talking about death and dying.

As expected, news of Andrea's failed attempt was somewhat awkward for everyone involved who assumed she had passed. I recalled a similar feeling back when I miscarried, and everyone assumed I was still pregnant. The difference was that Andrea's predicament wasn't discussed as much. Even medical professionals working in hospice care seemed ill-equipped to understand or problem-solve her particular situation, partly due to the risk of losing their licenses if they tried. Obviously, Washington state was off the table, as Seattle was completely overwhelmed with COVID-19. And the biggest irony of all, Death With Dignity – in any state – may not have worked at that point because it required the patient drink the medication, which Andrea's body couldn't absorb. Nobody seemed certain about whether a "back-up plan" was even legal in those cases because there's so much emphasis placed on the lethal drugs being self-administered without staff involvement.

When we announced Andrea's failed attempt on her private Facebook page, we were encouraged by the outpouring of compassion, sympathy, and support. Below is a small sampling of the comments.

- Kayt: "I'm in on championing Andrea's Death with Dignity Law here in AK!"
- Noel: "If you wish to pursue Andrea's Law, I would be happy to help with it as much as I could!"
- Ellis: "This is the best and worst post!!! I am so HAPPY AND THRILLED SHE GOT TO HAVE FUN. I am saddened that she didn't get the death with dignity she deserves! If you choose to pursue Andrea's Law, I will be here to support it in EVERY WAY."
- Carrie: "I am definitely on board with death with dignity for Andrea Law."
- Lesa: "I will support Andrea's Law!"
- Gabby: "It really was a rockstar style celebration of life, although there were many tears, we all made some amazing moments together as one big adopted family. I will fight like hell, like she has in this cancer process, to get an DWD law enacted in Alaska. People should not have to have make decisions like this without medical staff present so everything goes smoothly. I know she had a hell of a hangover the next day, but my gawd, we ALL partied like rockstars with her that night. It became a celebration of life for her, surrounded by people close to her.... the memories made that night will forever be in my heart."
- Danny: "She will always be the best rockstar we all know. I would definitely back the idea of championing the law as well. I'm glad she was able to experience some type of happiness even if it was only for a few hours. That's the moments

we should cherish and remember her as when she was most happy."

- Marsha: "It breaks my heart that she is still suffering. Her bravery is commendable. Sorry it failed."
- Heather: "I'm sad things didn't work out like planned, but I'm also happy she got to live so much in one night. Too bad they can't give her IV morphine... death with dignity needs to be nationwide!"
- Hayden: "If you decide to fight for Andrea's Law, your posts in this private group could be a brilliant weapon. Laws don't change unless hearts change, and hearts don't change without stories. Your openness and honesty in these posts will help you tell Andrea's story, if/when you ever want to. Thank you for including so many of us in this journey. I am ready to fight alongside you!"
- Carmen: "This is a subject that should be discussed and a law put into effect! I agree calling it Andrea's Law. No human deserves to be tortured this way — especially at the end of their time here on earth! It is cruel she has to go through this sxxt! However, her celebration of life party sounds great. I am so glad she was able to really party!! We're in your corner, you dearest people!!"
- ST: "Now we know why Andrea is still with us – to see Trump be felled by that which he mocked! Even if she may not be with us to see his political demise, she can know that karma does exist!"
- Souz: "Thank you so much for sharing the terrible and painful details about what Andrea is going through. I can only imagine how difficult it is to live this, let alone write about it! These things aren't often talked about, so I appreciate you helping to normalize these types of discussions. My heart breaks for you, Andrea, and all that love her."

I thanked people for acknowledging how hard it was to experience and write about. I believed it was important to help normalize talking about it and offer more exposure to exactly what was entailed for those suffering from chronic or terminal illnesses. I felt like I'd gotten a crash course and wish I'd known more before going into our nightmare. I started telling people, "After what I've witnessed in the U.S. healthcare system over the last 3 years, there's no way I'm going to be old, sick, or die in this country." Meanwhile, Sine completed a second set of artwork.

Tethered

Andrea's pain and suffering were intolerable, and she longed for Death with Dignity. Because Alaska does not allow physician assisted suicide, Andrea was forced to craft her own solution. Tragically, her courageous attempt to end her life through morphine failed because her cancer was too far progressed to allow the drugs to work. In this drawing, I imagine that she is tethered to this Earthly Realm.

Anahita

Please Take me With You

Andrea's middle name was Raven. After the drugs failed to
work, I imagined that she longed to fly away with the Ravens, to
leave life behind, and to return to Energy.

After realizing that Andrea's GI tract was unable to absorb anything, I became less militant about maintaining absolute compli-
ance with her medication regimen. Even 900mg capsules of RSO
had no effect on her. We continued Norco and liquid Morphine,
but they had little effect, which meant she was suffering. She really needed to be in a dedicated hospice facility that could administer pain medication via IV, but that option didn't exist in
Fairbanks at that time. State law required that any IV medications
must be continuously monitored by an RN onsite, which simply
wasn't feasible with the caseload that hospice nurses were carry-
ing. I imagined myself in their shoes, knowing that they couldn't
offer the care that they knew their patients needed. What a ter-

rible situation to be in, knowing your license was in jeopardy if you helped people in ways outside the law's restraints, even when it was desperately needed and wanted. I imagined how much suffering could've been avoided by patients and their families, just like us, if there were other options. I wondered how many other people had been in our shoes. Surely, there must have been somebody out there who had experienced something similar. In fact, Andrea asked hospice nurses about that specifically. Fearing repercussions, the nurses said they weren't allowed to talk about it, except to say that Andrea wasn't the only one.

A couple days after her failed attempt, Andrea got a visit from another hospice nurse and Andrea explained to her that she had come up with two more plans. The first involved sending me out to find street drugs (heroin) that she could inject. "But" she said, "I can't do that to Melanie; she wouldn't even know where to start." The second involved a firearm – to which the nurse had an immediate and strong reaction that Andrea didn't expect. Basically, the nurse explained, any time someone died that way, it forced hospice to call in a special clean-up team and launch an investigation. "Please," the nurse begged, "don't do that to me. It's so messy, and it's so much paperwork!" Thankfully, we were all saved by the bell in that moment because Andrea's daughter had just arrived with her boyfriend. They told Andrea they had something special to tell her, and something very special to ask her. So, Andrea put aside her planning to listen to her daughter. After a moment of fumbling, Andrea's daughter asked her boyfriend to speak instead. He explained that they had decided to get married, and they asked if Andrea would officiate their wedding ceremony! As we all started crying, Andrea nodded in the affirmative. "Of course," she whispered.

With a renewed sense of purpose, we all worked together to set up a plan to help Andrea make it long enough for the necessary legal paperwork to be processed. Andrea's daughter and her fiancé outlined the tasks they were completing while Andrea and I discussed her goals with a nurse. Having recently navigated the legal parts of our own wedding, I offered insights needed to complete our mission. One of the nurses said that normally they weren't allowed to prolong death, but that making it to her daughter's wedding was a worthy goal, a final wish that seemed very reasonable. One nurse made a plan to come administer IV fluids every other day for the following week. She also explained to Andrea that the only pain management option she had left was to administer liquid morphine rectally. At that point, sublingual wasn't doing enough. So, a nurse ordered a device that's normally used to administer medications vaginally, but instead, she would use it to administer rectally, calling it a rectal catheter. She showed me how to insert it and how to administer the liquid morphine. Then it was up to me to make sure the doses were given every 4 hours. Already exhausted, I realized I'd need to recruit help. So, over the following week, we set up shifts. Friends, family, and death doulas came and went in shifts to ensure Andrea was administered morphine rectally every 4 hours. We just needed to make it to her daughter's wedding!

By October 5, the day of the wedding, pretty much all of Andrea's dignity was gone. But at least she'd held on long enough to officiate her daughter's wedding ceremony – all thanks to hospice staff and various volunteers who pulled every string to make it happen! Andrea was very weak, and she struggled to read the words I'd printed out in large font for her. So, I read the officiating language aloud and then Andrea repeated them the best she could. I'm sure it's not how her daughter had dreamed of her wedding, but she said it was more important to her that Andrea was part of it. With tears in her eyes, Andrea told her new son-in-law that she could die at peace knowing he would take care of her daughter.

Andrea was struggling with multiple issues (lack of nutrition/starvation, lack of fluid intake/dehydration, pain, anxiety, and intestinal blockage). Even with all the meds onboard, both orally and rectally, Andrea was still battling heartburn/acid reflux and had several days of vomiting. Then, everything stopped. At Andrea's request, her daughter was sneaking in McDonalds. She would have never asked me because I have a particular disdain for fast food after reading "Fast Food Nation" while I was in graduate school. I see the whole operation as exploitation. McDonalds was Andrea's attempt to make herself vomit or poop, but it proved to be unsuccessful. Her GI tract had shut down. And the rectal catheter was becoming more and more difficult to reinsert. I really depended on Andrea's help to guide it around her rectal tumors and prolapsed rectal tissue. I was afraid there might come a point where neither of us could get it back in place. We tried to leave the rectal catheter in, but it fell out every time she went to the bathroom. When she urinated, it triggered rectal spasms and muscle contractions as if having a bowel movement which pushed the catheter out. Without the rectal catheter, we'd be out of options to administer medications. By the day after her daughter's wedding, Andrea had gone 9 days without nutrition and had only swallowed small amounts of water/ice. Both death doulas continued to take shifts sitting with her periodically to give me opportunities to rest. Andrea expressed to all of us that she just hoped she could vote before she passed. We'd heard that absentee ballots were starting to arrive in mailboxes (many people voted by mail during COVID), so we held out hope that another final wish might come true.

Meanwhile, one of the hospice nurses had found out that the closest pharmacy that offered IV drips for in-home use was in Anchorage – six hours away. They got most of their supply from Seattle (a COVID hotspot at the time). Unfortunately, Fairbanks was also severely limited in that type of service, and they didn't really have an inpatient option for Andrea at the local hospital either. Sadly, the funding from the community just wasn't there. Ten years prior, there was no hospice in Fairbanks at all – only volunteer services with very limited medical services. "It's grown lots since that time, but we still have a long way to go," the nurse said, "After Covid, I am just glad there is still a hospital here at all!"

A friend of mine from the dance community had just lost her husband to pancreatic cancer. She told me that not being able to give IV meds in the home setting was what made them decide to admit him to a hospice facility in another state. His pain had become unbearable, and he was no longer able to take anything orally, not even water. She couldn't bear to see him suffer. She was sad that he'd had to die in a hospice facility, but she was glad that he had his pain managed and it allowed her to spend his final day with him as a spouse, not as a caregiver. "I lay with him, sang to him, played music for him, and just soaked in the essence of him," she said, "I knew the hospice nurses had everything under control and that freed me from all but just loving him. It was not our original plan, but he passed very peacefully, and for that I am grateful." Unfortunately, we didn't have that option in Fairbanks; inpatient hospice care didn't exist yet. That meant Andrea was doomed to suffer. I told Andrea that if I could take some of her misery from her, I would. She replied, "I wouldn't wish this on my worst enemy."

CHAPTER 8: INFINITY

Much to everyone's surprise, Andrea lasted another 10 days after her daughter's wedding. But they were not good days. Andrea was basically skin and bones – like those pictures of holocaust survivors. At that point, there was no quality of life, and she considered it inhumane to suffer any additional quantity. As her spouse and caregiver, this was torture for me to watch. Death by cancer has been described as a very slow car crash, and I felt completely helpless to stop it. One day, I admitted to Andrea, "I cry a lot when you're not looking." She replied, whispering, "Me too."

I was administering her medications every 3 hours – around the clock – via the rectal catheter. She knew the weight of caregiving for 3 years was now in a sprint to the finish line for me – and I was exhausted. Nurses said that would be the time they'd normally be sending in the hospice volunteers, but because of COVID, they weren't allowed. So, once again, COVID screwed us over. Thankfully, our good friends came up from Anchorage to relieve me of duty for 2 nights by taking over the medication schedule so I could finally get some sleep. For me, this was most needed and appreciated. For caregivers, offering to take their night shift is probably the best gift you could give.

Despite all the suffering and exhaustion, Andrea was proud that she was able to accomplish two very significant things: 1) officiate her daughter's marriage ceremony, and 2) complete her absentee ballot for the general election – neither of which would've been possible without the hospice nurses who truly went ABOVE AND BEYOND for Andrea in so many ways. Andrea called one of her hospice nurses "my savior." They had many tender moments together, human to human, learning from each other. Together, they also lamented their lack of options to end her suffering. "We're allowed to be compassionate to end the suffering of our pets, yet we can't award the same compassion to ourselves." Those words still haunt those of us who heard her say it.

It was distressing for Andrea to feel her body withering away. She was extremely weak, fatigued, needed assistance to sit or stand, and sometimes didn't even have enough energy to speak. She spent so much time in bed that she started developing bed sores. Due to tumor growth in her abdomen, she hadn't been able to keep down any nutrition for over two weeks and was barely holding down small amounts of water. This also meant that all her medications had to be given via the rectal catheter – which she hated. I knew it was already much worse than she wanted – but she was afraid to go through the psychological trauma she'd experienced the first time she'd tried to end her suffering (for fear of failing again). I wondered if she might be accepting the idea of slowly dehydrating and/or starving to death. I asked her if there was a "deal breaker" – a point at which she considered it to be unacceptable suffering. She replied, "We're already way past that." She said she was experiencing exactly what she had wanted to avoid – then told me, "Tell everyone I don't recommend starving to death."

Finally, Andrea decided she had done all the things that mattered and that her suffering needed to end. She picked a day. When I asked why she picked that particular day, she said, "Because my daughter won't have to go to work the next day." Even in her final days, she worried about disrupting her daughter's life and planned based on days she knew her daughter was off work. She asked me to help her take one last shower, to comb her hair, and put on clean clothes – a monumental feat that took half the day. She was so weak and frail. I was shocked by the condition of her naked body barely standing in the shower, as if she would crumble and fall down the drain along with the water. Back in the hospital bed, she thanked me for helping her. Then, looking around the room, she whispered to me, again, "I'm sorry I didn't finish the house."

The time had come. Andrea requested a few close loved ones to be present. She asked us to be peaceful and quiet during her passing. She had already discussed everything with the death doulas regarding her wishes. She asked all of us to please respect her decision. She had decided on a new plan, but she didn't have solid backup plans so that she could avoid repeating her first attempt failure. She believed that if she tripled the amount of liquid morphine of her first attempt, that would be enough to end her suffering. Since she couldn't swallow anything, she decided the full amount would need to be administered in her rectal catheter.

Andrea spent time snuggling with our sweet kitty, Squirrel. They had a very special bond. Because of changes that I noticed in her behavior, I believed Squirrel knew something was happening with Andrea. Animals can sense things. Squirrel could sense that Andrea was saying goodbye and thanking her for being the best emotional support kitty ever. Then, just before Andrea carried out her plans, I tearfully read her this message as my goodbye:
"Dear Andrea,
You showed me how to break gender norms, that anyone can LEARN anything, BE anything, DO anything, even build houses. You showed me love, compassion, understanding, strength, brav-

ery, and communication. I am grateful for the time we had together. Thank you for being my soulmate. And as soulmates, I hope our atoms meet up again someday in this fucked up universe somewhere, somehow. Please know that I will always love you."

After many hugs and tears, Andrea began her plan. The process took much longer than anyone expected. Because of her rectal tumors, the catheter was always difficult to get into place. But this last attempt to get it in place was especially awful because Andrea was so weak and had no strength to maneuver it into position. She wanted to spare me from being involved, so she insisted on doing it independently. After struggling for far too long, she eventually asked me for help. Together, we finally got the catheter around the tumors. Andrea administered the full amount of liquid morphine into her rectum. For anyone else, that would have had an instant effect. But because cancer had completely taken over her colon, nothing happened. She held the liquid in for as long as she could, struggling to fight the urge to release it. Like an enema, it's only a matter of time before it comes out. Andrea was able to hold it for 15 minutes, which is a surprising amount of time. But again, nothing happened. Toward the end of that 15 minutes, she asked me to take a picture of her skinny arm with her son-in-law's watch on and text it to one of the hospice nurses. It was her way of sending the message that she was STILL waiting for death. The nurse was shocked that Andrea was still conscious.

Unable to hold it in any longer, all 90 milligrams of liquid morphine ended up in the toilet. Andrea felt so defeated, sad, and upset. Desperately, Andrea asked the nurse what else she could do. The nurse replied, "I don't know." I asked the nurse if she would come over to at least access Andrea's chemo port. I'd been forbidden from learning how to do it, so I'd never tried. But I figured that port would be Andrea's only avenue since she'd already ruled out oral and rectal. The nurse explained that she could only come over if Andrea was having a medical emergency. So, I called the hospice emergency number and said that Andrea was experiencing an uncontrolled pain episode and requested they send a nurse over. When the nurse arrived at our house, she talked with Andrea about everything she'd done to try to end her suffering and realized we were all out of options. Then, someone with medical training explained to me that there was usually an emergency kit that was stashed away with all the other medical supplies that hospice had initially brought into our home. They asked me where those supplies had been placed, and I pointed across the room to the desk that was piled with items that had been brought in by various staff. With no medical training, I had no knowledge of the contents nor use of most of the supplies in that pile. But the person with medical training quickly located the emergency kit and explained that it was only used during extreme anxiety or pain episodes that required IV administration, meaning a nurse must be present. However, in Andrea's case, with no other options allowed by hospice staff, we'd be on our own.

After Andrea's chemo port was accessed, the person with medical training explained to me how to use the supplies in the emergency kit. I recognized one of the drug names (Ativan), but the rest were foreign to me. Everything was pre-measured doses of liquid medication in individual syringes – without needles – just screw tips. I asked how much to add to the line going into Andrea's port; the person with medical training replied, "Everything." Then I was told that the nurse was leaving our house because she wasn't allowed to be present if the patient chooses to use medications in a way that differs from the way they were initially prescribed. So, after she left, I asked Andrea if she wanted to add the medications to her port herself. Exhausted, she asked me if I would please do it for her. "But" she pleaded, "just don't let me wake up."

With her permission, I began to add the medications to her port line. Andrea was able to eat a couple bites of pizza just before going unconscious. I saw her starting to slip into unconsciousness and I said "I love you" one last time. Her last words were, "I love you, too." After adding all the medications, I assumed it would be sufficient to accomplish her goal. But several hours later, she was still breathing. There were signs of overdose, like foaming at her mouth and changes to the sound of her breathing, but that didn't last long. After a few hours, I could tell she was starting to come back. The medications were wearing off. Afraid to let Andrea down, I contacted the nurse again to ask what to do. Even though it was late, the nurse said she would come over again to re-evaluate the situation.

By this time, most everyone in the house was asleep. When the nurse returned and evaluated Andrea, she remarked that "her healthy heart and lungs" were keeping her alive. Then, she did some calculations to determine the length of time since administering the medications and concluded that they were past their half-life, meaning that Andrea was on her way to waking up – again. Panicked, I said, "But I promised her she wouldn't wake up." I looked desperately into the nurse's face, searching for any hint of what I could do to help. She appeared unsure, but I believed she genuinely had compassion for our awful predicament. Perplexed, we sat silently in the dimly lit room, next to Andrea's bed. As I wiped tears from my eyes, the person with medical training was looking up something on their phone. In the silence, they slowly turned their phone toward me. The screen was filled with text – medical jargon that I didn't recognize – except for one word: air. I looked up and asked, "How much?" and they replied, "As much as it takes." Before they left the room, they looked back at me and asked, "Can you do it?" and I said, "Yes."

In that moment, I felt like my whole life had led me to do this one act of mercy for the fellow human I loved most. I knew it's what she wanted me to do. And I knew for certain that she would've done the same for me if the roles were reversed. So, I found one of the empty syringes and pulled back the plunger to fill it with air, then pushed it into Andrea's port line. I repeated that a few more times until her breathing slowed. Then, Andrea's Native American ancestors came to take her to the lights. Our friend Kale took a photo of the Northern Lights from above the city as Andrea was passing. I'd lived in Alaska for 15 years and had never seen such an amazing display. It was breathtaking – literally. Andrea stopped breathing and I could tell she was gone. It was a humbling moment. But I was so thankful her suffering was finally over and that her wishes were honored. I woke up Andrea's daughter and told her Andrea was gone. She looked at me and nodded her head.

Just after midnight, the nurse came to give the official pronouncement of death and called the funeral home to give the proper information. We took turns going outside, eyes skyward, to witness the spectacular Aurora show above our house. As her closest loved ones, with the nurse to help guide us, we took the time to carefully wash and dress Andrea's body. As requested, her final outfit was all purple – including the "FUCK CANCER" T-shirt made by a friend. Then, as requested, I took off her wedding ring, and mine, and placed our rings on either side of the necklace to symbolize that cancer had separated us. The nurse left but said we could take all the time we needed before calling the funeral home for pickup. Since there would be no memorial service or funeral, this was our only chance to say goodbye. I called to notify people on Andrea's list. Some people chose to come pay their final respects and others declined. Everyone deals with grief differently and I understood not everyone could handle seeing her body, whereas others needed the experience.

I couldn't believe how beautiful and peaceful Andrea looked. I told her how beautiful she was, repeatedly. She seemed so peaceful after her suffering was over. I laid next to her body for a long time until I started nodding off. Then, Squirrel took over. She patiently kept vigil over Andrea's body until the sun came up, curled up on the chair beside Andrea's bed. I woke up to Squirrel still sitting next to Andrea. I remembered the nurse said we were only allowed 12 hours with the body, and I panicked that noon was soon approaching. I wasn't ready. I wanted more time. It was hard to leave her bedside when the funeral home came to take her body. I'm glad I had people with me when that happened because it was WAY harder than I thought it would be. I was not prepared for that. It just felt so final, watching them drive away with her body, knowing I'd never see her again. That was the worst part for me.

For Squirrel, too, the worst part was when they took Andrea's body away. There was a heartbreaking moment when Squirrel let out the saddest concerned meows I'd ever heard her make. I ran to find her immediately. She was on the bed looking around searching for Andrea. I sat down with her and told her that Andrea was gone but that it was okay to be sad. Then I held her in my arms and cried – a lot. Later, the hospital came to pick up all the home medical equipment – but Squirrel didn't want them to take the bed! Shortly after Andrea's body was taken, I made a short announcement post on Andrea's private Facebook group to let everyone know of her passing, which elicited some of the most beautiful comments from friends who loved us. Below is a small sampling of them.

- Alex: "I'm so glad her suffering is over. Thank you for trusting me to hold space with you over the past twenty days. It was an honor to be present in these moments and I will forever be grateful for the conversations Andrea and I shared — and that last joint while listening to Jon Bon Jovi this morning. Seeing the relief on her face was so bittersweet. I love you so much! FUCK CANCER."
- Gabby: "It was bittersweet to see Andrea's body finally relaxed, not in pain and peaceful. An odd sense of calm happened last night while the lights danced above. Even in your suffering, you loved unconditionally."
- Taylor: "I am grateful that you two found each other, and that Andrea knew true love and acceptance in you before one of life's cruelest circumstances took her from us all. I am grateful for the opportunity to assist you in any way that I can. Most of all, I am grateful that her pain and suffering is at an end; she was too beautiful a soul to have gone through what she did, but she had the great fortune of having you at her side."
- Morgan: "You are and have been so immensely strong through all of this; It's been heroic."
- Kiara: "She was and is one of the most amazingly intellectual, kind, funny, talented, pyre of strength badass human beings that I have ever been lucky enough to have in my presence. I am so thankful for her and the time that I was gifted with her before she broke free from the terrible shell her magnificent spirit had been trapped in. You are strong and have so much to teach, that you taught with her, and will continue to teach for her. The lights came to welcome her into the great cosmic sky."

That first night alone, without Andrea, I had so many thoughts and emotions to process, just trying to make sense of everything.

I looked around at our house and remembered all the time, love, and memories we'd made there. I remembered Andrea had taken a picture of me in 2014 while we were building our house together – standing in the same room where all our hopes and dreams were woven, then unraveled. Little did I know that would be the same room where Andrea and I would get married, where her daughter would get married, and where she would die – all within 10 weeks. Our still unfinished house was a tangible representation of the unfinished life that cancer stole from us.

Andrea's daughter pointed out to me that Andrea died on 10/17, which was Andrea's last message to us (10+17=27) because 27 means "I love you" in the language that they had with each other. That explained why she waited until just after midnight to return to the cosmos – and such a stereotypical Andrea thing to do! After getting her daughter's permission, I submitted Andrea's obituary the following day to be published in the Fairbanks News Miner: Andrea Raven Taylor died peacefully on October 17, 2020, at the age of 45 in Fairbanks, Alaska. She was born on April 16, 1975, in Port Huron, Michigan, but lived in Alaska for 31 years (since 1989). She loved music, played guitar most of her life, and had a career in Information Technology; but her greatest achievement was raising an amazing daughter – her reason for living. Andrea bravely battled cancer for 3 years, showing us all her fighting spirit. She will be deeply missed by family and friends who will carry her memory in their hearts. Andrea was survived by her spouse, Melanie Lindholm, her parents, her brothers, and her daughter. She was preceded in death by her grandparents. Memorial contributions may be made to the Fairbanks North Star Borough Animal Shelter. No services will be held. Condolences may be made to the family at Blanchardfamilyfuneralhome.com.

Because of our cosmic, other worldly connection as soulmates, I knew Andrea wasn't truly gone. The atoms that made her body still existed, and the beauty of her consciousness was in the Northern Lights with her Native American ancestors. We both believed in science, the wonders of the universe, and the connection between all things, both living and dead. For me, this is perhaps best described by the physicist Aaron Freemen:

"You want a physicist to speak at your funeral. You want the physicist to talk to your grieving family about the conservation of energy, so they will understand that your energy has not died. You want the physicist to remind your sobbing mother about the first law of thermodynamics; that no energy gets created in the universe, and none is destroyed. You want your mother to know that all your energy, every vibration, every Btu of heat, every wave of every particle that was her beloved child remains with her in this world. You want the physicist to tell your weeping father that amid energies of the cosmos, you gave as good as you got. And at one point, you'd hope that the physicist would step down from the pulpit and walk to your brokenhearted spouse there in the pew and tell them that all the photons that ever bounced off your face, all the particles whose paths were interrupted by your smile, by the touch of your hair, hundreds of trillions of particles, have raced off like children, their ways forever changed by you. And as your widow rocks in the arms of a loving family, may the physicist let her know that all the photons that bounced from you were gathered in the particle detectors that are her eyes, that those photons created within her constellations of electromagnetically charged neurons whose energy will go on forever. You can hope your family will examine the evidence and satisfy themselves that the science is sound and that they'll be comforted to know your energy's still around. According to the law of the conservation of energy, not a bit of you is gone; you're just less orderly."

Then, beautifully, with the gift of art, Sine Anahita completed her series titled "Andrea's Final Journey" to illustrate this transition of energy in a way that forever honors her.

Andrea, the Ancestors have come
Finally, Death came. As she was leaving the planet, the aurora borealis danced overhead in a splendid array. Her Native American ancestors had come to take her away.

She loved purple best

Andrea loved all things purple. Here, I imagine her surrounded
by the spiritual energy embodied in purple flowers: wild violets,
lavender, crocus, pansies, orchids, and daisies.

A week after Andrea's death, Sine's art series went on display at the University of Alaska Fairbanks' Fine Arts Building. Sine's art professor put them on display, as he was very moved by the drawings. Of the experience, Sine said, "I was deeply honored by Andrea's willingness to let me chronicle her final journey, and grateful that she and you welcomed me into your home. She was a beautiful person and will always be my favorite model. I totally enjoyed getting to know her, and feel so blessed. Andrea faced Death with courage and resolve. I feel very honored that she invited me into her very private realm to chronicle her final journey. The experience of drawing her has changed me in ways that I have yet to understand. I feel that she is with us still, her Energy lingering, her passion for life, and her love for her family and friends still pouring forth. All of us who knew her are truly blessed." Indeed, many other loved ones remarked at the beauty of the artwork, how it uniquely captured Andrea's journey, and shone a light on Alaska's dire need for Death With Dignity legislation so that nobody else would be forced to suffer like Andrea did. In fact, Andrea explicitly stated that she didn't want anyone to repeat her experience.

After their display on campus, Sine offered to have her artwork professionally framed to be donated to the hospice office for permanent display. I made a presentation in front of hospice staff to present the framed art and to tell Andrea's story. I was nervous about being so emotional in front of people, but mostly, I was worried about doing it justice. I wanted to honor Andrea, her journey, Sine's art, and to tell the story – so that everyone in the building would recognize their significance. After my presentation, the staff who had been part of Andrea's team thanked me and then asked me to also tell the story of Squirrel, the cutest emotional support kitty ever. When the building staff finished hanging the art, I went back to see for myself, to witness "Andrea's Final Journey" officially on display in their permanent home. Then I cried like a baby in my car so nobody would see me. To my knowledge, the art series is still on display at the Hospice Services building in Fairbanks, Alaska.

Years later, in Canada, I gave a similar presentation in a grief support group when I was given the opportunity to tell Andrea's story. I showed pictures and explained her struggle with cancer. I used Sine's artwork series to open the discussion about Death With Dignity. Being Canadians, the group members were horrified and shocked by the lack of options available to Andrea in Alaska. I explained that was one of the reasons Andrea made me promise to move – because Canada has universal MAID (medical aid in dying). She wanted me to have more options than she had – in case I was ever in her shoes. And by telling her story, I was also honoring another promise I made to her. The group was especially amazed by Andrea's beauty, our house's purpleness, and Squirrel's cuteness. Telling Andrea's story, both oral and written, has helped me process it and put things in perspective. Being open and brutally honest about what we went through together is the best way for me to honor Andrea.

Near the end of October 2020, Andrea's daughter and her husband went with me to pick up Andrea's ashes. I was so glad we went together because I couldn't have done it by myself – the grief was too raw and painful – and I couldn't stop the tears. Andrea had chosen a purple biodegradable urn because she'd requested that her daughter and I take her ashes to the ocean together someday. Andrea also requested that we mix her ashes with the ashes of her sweet 20-year-old kitty, Tigerlilly. So, Andrea's daughter and I got together to mix the ashes and to also put a small amount in our necklaces. I was so grateful to receive a custom-made gift from an artist affiliated with Access Alaska to hold Andrea's ashes that included two hearts, star, moon, feathers, and a string of ocean-colored beads. It mirrored so many elements of Andrea's essence along with our longstanding representation of two hearts intertwined in the infinity symbol (like the rings we wore for so many years). We'd always believed that we knew each other before this life and that we'd somehow be reunited after – not in a religious sense, but in a physical atomic sense. Andrea constantly told me, "I love you – times infinity." But if I ever said the exact same thing, she'd counter with, "Well, I love you – times infinity – plus one." I'd always argue that it was mathematically impossible to add one to infinity, but she insisted that she'd always one-up me. "I love you the most – times infinity – so there – the end."

CHAPTER 9: MY GRIEF

The best advice I received at the beginning of grieving Andrea's passing came from another woman who'd also lost her wife to a terminal illness: "Grief is felt by different people in different ways. Don't ever let anyone tell you how you should grieve or feel. You have gone through so much – both the ups and downs and valleys in between. Be kind to yourself and let yourself heal. Feel whatever you feel, and don't let anyone tell you otherwise." That one piece of advice – from someone who'd been in my shoes – gave me permission to feel a multitude of emotions that came up from inside me. But because of COVID, I didn't seek out grief counseling or grief support groups until months later. And, because Andrea died just before the holiday season, I was facing it without proper support. I admit, I drank more than I should have during November and December. Alcohol was a temporary way of coping, but I knew I'd need to get myself together in the new year. I'd promised Andrea I'd leave the U.S., and I couldn't let her down. Fortunately, by mid-January, my goal-oriented-self came back online, and I started donating or selling everything in the house.

In the meantime, I was also learning a lot about grief. From the words of Chaplain David Rumph, I learned that the word "grief" was based on the Latin word gravare, which means "heavy," and that the heaviness of a broken heart is an instinctive human response to loss. Grief is normal, natural, and necessary. It is not something to be ashamed of. Grief is, in fact, a healthy reaction to the loss of someone we love. Grief is the price we pay for love. The only cure for grief is to grieve. We don't "recover from" or "get over" grief. Instead, we become reconciled to it, learning to live with it. The only way forward is through. Further, because love and grief are intimately related and because love never ends, grief never ends either. Although reconciliation is the goal, it is never a "finish line." The debilitating heartache remains, slowly diminishing over time, eventually allowing for hope and joy again, each in their own way. Over time, our capacity to hold our grief grows – and allows us to slowly live our life again.

For me, grief came in waves. Sometimes the wave gently licked the shore, and other times it was a tsunami that knocked me out. It was a good thing Gabby gave me a Costco case of Kleenex! I thought I was okay one minute, then I'd be back to crying like a baby the next. Logically, my brain understood that Andrea's suffering had ended, but my heart didn't understand why losing her hurt so much! I had to accept that my grief would last a very long time, perhaps until my own death. But I decided to let it be what it needed to be and to take all the time I needed. Andrea told me that she wanted me to find happiness and to live my life, but I didn't know how I was going to do that without her. As I discovered, I would never really be done grieving; it would just evolve over time.

In the weeks and months following her death, I thought about all the people who had been touched by Andrea's life, and I invited some of them to share their thoughts so I could post them on her private page for all of us grieving to find comfort in their words. The first was Lane, a friend who had applied to medical school. Andrea told Lane that if he was going to become a doctor to improve lives, then he also needed to understand what happens at the end of life. I asked Lane to write about how Andrea impacted him, and this is what he shared:

Andrea had a significant impact on my life. This impact began before I met her, and it will last throughout my life. Andrea is a positive and optimistic person. Even after three years of suffering from cancer, she still had a cheerful and contagious smile. I wrote down the words with warmth and a smile, and I knew she would like her friends to miss her like this. The quality of life lies not in length but dimensions. If my life was three-dimensional before Andrea showed up, then my life became six-dimensional after she appeared. The story of her living a true self inspires me to accept myself and be myself bravely, finally. When I was depressed and confused, she told me to strengthen my faith and not live for others. She knew that I wanted to be a doctor, then let me touch her cancerous part, told me the whole cancer experience, and allowed me to be by her side when she died. Andrea was humorous, unrestrained, had a clear view of what she wanted. She is an exquisite person in her bones. Even when approaching death, she still asked me whether seeing her costs me too much time. My friend, you really think about others too much. At this moment, you can do whatever you want, and I am willing to spend whatever much time with you. It was my honor to be with you in the last moments of your life. I am very grateful and will always remember the warmth and strength you gave me through your hand when you were dying, and I will bring them to more people.

Indeed, many people had been touched by Andrea, even while she was dying. As hard as it was for me and others to write about, those who read our words thanked us for sharing and allowing them to be part of the journey. But I'd had a 3-year head start on most people, as I'd been grieving since Andrea's diagnosis. I grieved every step of the way as cancer stole each part of our lives from us. It was hard to describe the desperation we felt as our hopes and dreams together were slowly taken away. While death brings a certain amount of relief from the grueling suffering, it also brings sadness on a level that was impossible for my heart to process. Relief that Andrea was no longer suffering was such a contradiction to the agony in my heart. I was grieving all the plans we had – and all the years we thought we'd have.

However, my grief was not one of regrets – because I knew I did everything I could possibly do and gave all the love I could give. Instead, my grief was mourning for the loss of the life we thought we'd live together and being haunted by what we'd built together – that now seemed so empty. Multiple times a day I entered the room where she'd spent the last months of her life struggling, the same room where she died. That room was unfinished, just like her life. Cancer stole our ability to finish our house, our dreams, and our lives together. One night, I stood in that room, remembering her laying there, everything we'd suffered through, but how our love for each other never wavered. I talked to the empty space where her energy had left her body. I said how much I missed her, how much I loved her, how I hoped her energy was learning new and wonderful things. I wished I could just hug her, hold her, cry with her. But the closest I could get was to hold her container of ashes against my chest, rocking back and forth, crying on the floor of our closet.

I had rough days and less rough days. Even though I knew for a long time that her death was coming, it was still hard to deal with after it happened. Logically, everything made sense. Emotionally, everything hurt. It was a strange place to be. And living in our house, being constantly reminded of her, might have been good for grieving – but it was bad for moving forward. I felt it would be best for me to sell the house, move to Canada, and start my life over (again). Andrea had already approved of this plan and made me promise I'd try to be happy. I desperately wanted to honor that promise, but grief was holding me back – and would for a long time.

On top of grief, I was angry. Two weeks after her death, Social Security retracted Andrea's October disability benefit without no-tification. After inquiry, I found out that the person receiving the disability benefit must be alive the entire month to keep that month's disbursement. So, not only had I lost my PCA/DSP job in August (because we got married) but then I also lost our primary household income (SSDI) in September. Although I was still work-ing my other job, there was no way I could pay for heat and other utilities for the rest of winter. Also, I got a check for $187 from Social Security as the "standard death benefit" – and that was all I was entitled to. Since we hadn't been legally married for more than 6 months, I wasn't eligible for any spouse's benefits. (We'd been living as if we were married for 8 years, but Alaska doesn't recognize common law marriage). Justifiably, I had a lot of anger. I was mad that cancer had destroyed us both financially. I was mad that cancer and chemo had destroyed Andrea's body. I was mad that the U.S. healthcare system values profits over people, that we'd been forced to fight that system the entire way. I was mad that the State of Alaska didn't have any Death With Dignity op-tions for her. I was mad that Social Security did nothing – aside from $187 – to support me as I'm grieving the loss of my spouse. When I needed it most, I'd lost the majority of our household in-come and was denied spouse's benefits entirely – all because I'd chosen to care for my sick loved one.

It was impossible to cremate Andrea with just $187. Thankfully, friends and family chipped in to cover the $2,300 required. And it was impossible to cover utilities during the winter for me to continue living in our house with just one job. Thankfully, our dear Anchorage friends came to my rescue; they covered months of heating and other utilities until I could get the house on the market in the spring. I will be eternally grateful for their help and hope I'll be able to repay them someday. Because Andrea had no life insurance, the only asset was our unfinished house. However, I'd already been warned it would be difficult to sell an unfinished house. Indeed, it turned out to be a long messy process. From the time it went on the market to the final sale was 2.5 years.

Rightly so, I also had plenty of anger about COVID. Although it didn't kill her, COVID affected Andrea's last months of life and the decisions she was forced to make about her death. Her plan was to pursue Death With Dignity in Seattle, but COVID curtailed travel and overwhelmed Washington state's healthcare system. COVID deprived her of her final wishes for her death. Her plan was to throw a large Celebration of Life party but COVID limited group sizes, activities, and venues. Andrea wanted to do so much more with so many people, but due to the pandemic, we had to severely limit visits from family/friends. COVID deprived her of seeing all her friends before she died. COVID deprived her of saying goodbye. COVID deprived us of additional support during the dying process because hospice volunteers weren't allowed to come over. I grieved the injustice of it all. Andrea didn't deserve cancer, suffering, starvation, and lack of choices. I didn't deserve bankruptcy or watching her suffer and die.

When it came to grief, my pain was as exquisite as our love. The depth of my sorrow was equal to the depth of our souls. My heart was raw, broken and bleeding. But it was only because our love and connection were so beautiful. I embraced the saying: "'Tis better to have loved and lost – than to have never loved at all." I began to fully appreciate and honor my grief as a form of gratitude. I was fortunate to have met Andrea, to be loved by her, to be part of her journey, to experience triumphs and tragedies alongside her. Of all the people in the universe, I was the one who'd had that fortune.

A month after Andrea's death was her daughter's birthday. Knowing she wouldn't make it, I'd preemptively gotten Andrea to sign birthday and Christmas cards for her daughter. On the appropriate days, I gave the cards to her daughter on Andrea's behalf. Andrea had also made a voice recording and instructed me to play it for her daughter on her birthday. We were all in tears when Andrea's daughter opened her card and listened to Andrea's voice recording. Andrea's daughter posted, "My first birthday without her was difficult, as is every day that has passed without her light. Still, she found a way to comfort me from beyond, and I am so fortunate to have had someone so special in my life. I'm always watching, listening, and waiting for you, Daddio." Of all of us, Andrea's daughter was the one that had the most dreams and visions of Andrea. Her daughter always had a special connection with Andrea, and that continued after her passing. Andrea sent many messages and signs to her daughter through her dreams. With me, it was mostly through premonitions while I was awake, but also through signs in nature, some using technology, and of course, music. Andrea definitely made it known that her energy was still around.

Although I did put up Andrea's Christmas tree, I spent most of December 2020 doing significant grieving, writing, reading, crying, and processing. I wasn't totally new to grief. I had experienced significant loss before: the "death" of my identity/life in a cult, the "death" of a previous 20-year marriage, and the literal death of dear pets. In my experience, the pain and grieving never disappeared; it only lessens over time. In the case of losing Andrea, I believed closure was never possible for me. In fact, the very idea that I could reach a point where I no longer missed Andrea was obscene to me. In my mind, true closure would imply something could be done to fix it, like some kind of justice, revenge, or restitution – none of which was possible with the kind of cancer that steals everything from you. I would always grieve what cancer stole from us. I didn't just grieve her death; I grieved the life we planned to live together. I accepted that my grief may lessen over time, but it would never be gone. And, in my case, closure wasn't the goal of grieving anyway. Grief just is what it is. I just chose to feel and think whatever feelings and thoughts came, without judgement or expectation. Everyone grieves in their own way and on varying timescales; that meant nobody could tell me how (or for how long) I grieved.

Also in December 2020, I fulfilled a promise I'd made to Andrea by getting my colon cancer screening (colonoscopy). I could still vividly remember Andrea's colonoscopy three years prior (when we first heard the "C" word), and I had flashbacks just walking into the waiting room. As I waited, I cried because I remembered being there with Andrea. Then I cried again when the nurse said she remembered Andrea. Thankfully, my screening results showed everything was normal. I told everyone to get their cancer screenings, too, as early detection is the key to survival.

Then, shortly after Christmas, Andrea's dad passed away after enduring terrible pain and agony. That meant the Taylor family was dealing with two deaths – two months apart – on top of the holidays, the pandemic, and the political stress. To perfectly sum up 2020, my sister-in-law said, "What the fuck, man. Fuck this year, dude." I couldn't have agreed more. It was a terrible year for so many people, for so many reasons. So, I took it upon myself to make a short post: "This is your reminder to be kind to yourself and others. Please honor Andrea by living and being happy – the two things she was cheated out of."

One of Andrea's music friends remarked: "Melanie, I think you have a profound and meaningful perspective on grief. Your communication has been fearless. I was moved by Andrea's long-standing courage." I agreed that Andrea had long-standing courage, certainly more than I could ever have. I was continually in awe of her ability to keep fighting. Three years of pain and suffering – much longer than I would've made it if I'd been in her shoes. Even with my perspective on grief, it still caught me off guard regularly. For instance, one day, my grief was triggered by gathering all my recyclables. I found several flattened boxes of Ensure – the only "food" that Andrea could tolerate in the last 3 months of her life. My obvious distress and tears alerted Squirrel who immediately came to offer comfort and support. Andrea's hospice support kitty had become my grief support kitty. I'd experienced a lot of changes, and I was still adjusting, grieving, and learning to live differently. I'd gone from round-the-clock caregiver to grieving widow overnight. I missed Andrea every day, but I was striving to honor my promises to her: to live and be happy. I was doing the best I could, but some days I just cried. As I continued clearing out our house, I fulfilled another promise to Andrea: to destroy 48 hard drives (from her many years of computer work). That was part of what I later called "my marching orders" including giving her electronic equipment to a friend, giving tools and construction supplies to other friends, giving her music equipment to her daughter, selling our house (we'd agreed that neither of us would live in it without the other), and leaving the U.S.

Andrea wanted her story told, and fortunately, Sine's artwork gave me an avenue to honor that. Sine helped pick out matts and frames for her artwork, then donated them to be displayed at the hospice office. She also gave me ownership and permission over their use – as well as offering prints to anyone who wanted them – at no charge. I was continuously in awe of Sine's gracious gift to Andrea and all who cared for her. With my permission, Sine sent the reproductions to anyone who requested them. My only request was that she also include the summary page of Andrea's Final Journey along with each print. It was a way to ensure Andrea's story was told in honor of her wishes. Fans of Sine's artwork requested prints – some of whom had never met Andrea. Friends and family considered Sine's artwork to be a beautiful tribute to the most courageous woman we knew. Andrea leaned into death with courage and grace. Admittedly, I had not been able to process my grief with the same grace. It was a rocky process for me, filled with mourning and sorrow, but also anger and frustration. Sine's artwork gave me words, a way to say them, and a way to be heard. Doing the presentation at hospice was one of the hardest but most fulfilling ways I'd had to express that. For me, telling Andrea's story was not only a way I honor her, but also a way for me to process my grief.

In January 2021, one of Andrea's death doulas – who had received a complete set of Sine's art series – made the following public post:

> These art pieces were presented to our local hospice office this week and will be on display. They were presented by the spouse of the subject in the artwork. The artwork was created by Dr. Sine Anahita in the final days of Andrea's life, and served to document the dying process, and its impact on Andrea. I was one of several team members who provided support to the family during Andrea's tumultuous dy-

ing process. This artwork is a testament to her bright spirit, and determination to live and die on her own terms. As a doula, I was incredibly impressed with the thought behind this artwork. It served as a legacy piece for Andrea, as well as a precious gift to her loved ones. I was honored to receive prints of this work, and it will serve as an excellent example for future clients for one of many ways we can try to move through death with depth, honor, and reverence. Andrea wanted her story told. This information and these photos and video have been shared with permission, both by Andrea before her death and by her spouse, Melanie.

Later, Access Alaska contacted me asking permission to use Andrea's story as a special feature in their annual agency report publication. Along with the artwork series, the following is what they published:

Andrea's Story

Access Alaska's Consumer Directed Care Service has the honor of serving individuals that fall across the spectrum of aging and disability. Direct Service Professionals work passionately to support individuals across the lifespan, including the final stages of life. With permission from her spouse, we would like to share Andrea's story. Andrea's desire was that her legacy continue by sharing her story and her belief that everyone deserves death with dignity.

Andrea and her fiancée, Melanie, became involved with Access Alaska during the summer of 2018. Melanie and Andrea shared that they had been working on building a home together and were living in their partially finished home when they had found out that Andrea had Stage IV colorectal cancer. They also shared that they had been engaged and had not found the right time to have the wedding they both dreamed of. Andrea exuded a certain strength, confidence, and fierceness. Andrea entered the PCA program that fall, and naturally her fiancée took on the role of caregiver.

Melanie was a strong advocate, partner, and caregiver—she played several roles that all required a great amount of strength. Andrea continued to fight her battle against cancer with Melanie as her round-the-clock caregiver. The pair expressed how exhausting it was to be battling an illness and simultaneously battling the healthcare system. They faced obstacles each time her insurance would make changes to what types of treatments would be covered, prescriptions she could receive, her ability to travel for treatment, or her right to die the way she chose.

Andrea battled cancer for three years and bravely endured 52 chemotherapy cycles. Then her cancer spread, and she could no longer endure the painful treatments. With her doctor's guidance, Andrea chose to end her cancer treatment and entered Hospice care in June 2020. As Andrea's health declined, the couple decided they had one thing left to do—get married. Melanie and Andrea had a beautiful wedding at home, clad in all things purple, and surrounded by close friends and family. Andrea passed peacefully at home this past October with her wife by her side.

Artist/photo credit:

Sine Anahita created the included illustrations chronicling Andrea's final journey. The original drawings are framed and hung in the FHP Hospice Services building for the public to view. More information about the artist can be found here: https://www.sineanahita.art/

A woman named Katrina who was Andrea's case manager at Access Alaska also requested prints of "Andrea's Final Journey" to be displayed in their new building. As it turned out, the new Access Alaska building was the same building that was formerly the

Gold Rush bar back when Andrea's band "Lucid" would play there (Andrea's daughter was also in the band). How ironic that "Andrea's Final Journey" would be hung in that same building! Katrina said the agency director specifically requested the one with ravens (Take Me With You) to be printed on the cover of their annual report. Apparently, he was very touched by that piece. This was not the first time Sine's artwork had made such an impression; even people who didn't know Andrea were taken aback by her story. While I was at the new Access Alaska building (former Gold Rush bar) to drop off the prints, Katrina and I were talking (we were the only ones in the building) and suddenly we heard a big crash sound from the medical equipment room, which was the same area the stage used to be. Katrina was really spooked, but I said, "Oh, that's probably just Andrea trying to f*ck with us." When I told Andrea's daughter about this, she said, "Yep, that's dad makin' music again!"

By early Spring of 2021, my grief had developed into a very painful condition called adhesive capsulitis, commonly known as "frozen shoulder." The OMM doctor treating me said that most people with the condition are middle-aged women with a history of significant emotional trauma. I told him that if that was true, then I was the perfect candidate. My doctor explained that not only is adhesive capsulitis very painful, but because it has roots in emotional trauma, it needed to be processed in multiple ways. So, I finally got a referral for grief counseling. Turns out, I couldn't deal with it by myself like I thought I could. I would be getting professional help – and I wasn't ashamed to admit it. I knew there was some societal stigma around seeking mental health care, but I couldn't let that hold me back anymore. One of Andrea's music friends told me: "Thank you for not being ashamed. No one should have to experience doubt or shame over wanting to know themselves better through the lens of an objective mental health professional. Andrea would not want you to suffer. The last thing Andrea ever sent me were the words: 'Life is too short to be miserable.' It impacted me deeply because I lost my father the week before. I needed help to be okay then, and now, and I truly hope you find peace and encouragement."

I spent the rest of spring and summer in grief counseling, OMM treatments, and physical therapy – all very painful – while continuing to work, putting the house on the market, moving my daughter to another place, and preparing to leave Alaska. In August 2021, I celebrated our first wedding anniversary by watching our wedding video, looking at our wedding album, eating cake, and drinking champagne. Also in August, on National Grief Awareness Day, I met Sine at the post office to send a small amount of Andrea's ashes to the glass artist who was making pendants for me, as well as Andrea's daughter and mother. I brought a box of tissues with me; I couldn't not cry. I missed her every day, but I knew she wanted me to try to live my life and be happy. I was desperately trying to honor her wishes. Andrea made me promise that I would go to Canada because she wanted me to have better options than she did (specifically universal healthcare and Medical Aid in Dying). I didn't have a disease nor plans to die. But Andrea died at age 45 and I was already 47, so I knew "shit happens." After witnessing what Andrea experienced, I refused to be sick, old, or die in the U.S. I was born with dual citizenship, so it made the most sense to move to Canada. Later, I learned that Canadians were generally appalled by the U.S. system. To them, it was shocking that the U.S. allowed so many citizens to go uninsured, that medical bankruptcies were commonplace, that people suffering with terminal illnesses were denied Death With Dignity options; Canadians consider it unethical and inhumane.

Reasons for me to move to Canada:
1. Universal healthcare
2. Universal legal cannabis
3. Universal Medical Aid in Dying (MAID)

In other words:
1. Nobody would be forced to file bankruptcy if I got cancer.
2. Nobody would have to illegally obtain cannabis for me if I got cancer.
3. Nobody would have to watch me die of cancer.

September 27, 2021 – the anniversary of Andrea's first attempt which ended up being her Celebration Of Life – was the day I left Alaska. Very fitting that was the day I honored my promise to her to start my new life in Canada. I felt her guiding me every step of the way. But there's a certain grief in learning to live again. I was leaving behind friends, family, dance troupe, the university community, the LGBTQ+ community, and the 17 years of life I'd lived in Fairbanks. I was going to another country, to a city where I didn't know anyone.

People asked me why I chose the province, the city, or the apartment that I did – and the answer was always "Andrea." She was the one who guided me in every decision. Just as one example: When I first arrived, Gabby asked me for my new mailing address. She put the address into Google Maps, went to street view, and took a screenshot to send me – because it was clearly a sign. There was a raven on the front lawn of the apartment building! Also, that apartment building ended up being just two blocks away from Nathan's house – the person I felt Andrea had chosen for me – whom I met just four days later. I met Nathan during the brief 48 hours that I was on Tinder, an app that a friend had encouraged me to try as a way to meet people as I started life in a new city. To me, the similarities between Andrea and Nathan were mind-blowing – so much so that I had to make a list to keep track of them all. There were 32 similarities on that list. To me, that couldn't be a coincidence. I knew Andrea had "set us up." Nathan came into my life because I had Andrea, and because I lost Andrea. She was always present in my relationship with Nathan – partly because Andrea's life, love, and death made me the kind of person that Nathan would want to be with. So, in short, I have not moved on from Andrea, but rather WE have moved forward WITH her.

On October 17, 2021, a year after Andrea's energy transitioned to another plane of existence, I honored her by lighting a purple candle and told her story to as many as would listen. She wanted her story told and I used Sine's artwork to do that. Andrea set me up to meet some very special people in British Columbia that I could share this with, surrounded by love and understanding. She truly wanted me to live my life and be happy – because she was making that happen.

Loving you
changed my life.

It should come as
no surprise
that losing you
has done the same.

—CHLOË FRAYNE.

CHAPTER 10: MY OWN CANCER

After my experience dealing with Andrea's cancer treatment and battling insurance in the U.S. healthcare system, I'd come to the conclusion that the entire thing was rigged. Big Pharma, insurance companies, Wall Street, the FDA, medical schools, and doctors were all part of a giant scam to make profits. Over time, any cure for cancer had been deliberately squashed. Absolutely nothing except 3 options (drugs, surgery, radiation) were approved by the FDA and billable for insurance reimbursement. Choosing any other treatment meant leaving the country and/or paying out-of-pocket. Americans were doomed to debilitating treatments while being sucked dry financially. With 1 in 3 Americans diagnosed with cancer in their life, most would deal with the rigged system in some way. In my opinion, making lucrative profits off sick and dying people was called extortion – and it was unethical, inhumane, and unacceptable.

Insurance premiums aren't used toward the customer's healthcare costs; they are used to pay lobbyists and investors. Even if you pay all your premiums, deductibles and co-pays, the insurance company can still refuse to pay what your doctor has ordered. And U.S. insurance can drop you without notice, then debt collections can hound you indefinitely to get you to pay. It happened to me. It's one of the reasons I left the country. Repeated and standard denials of insurance claims was one of the reasons people cheered the assassination of United Healthcare's millionaire CEO in late 2024.

Every American has experienced either being dropped from their insurance, having a claim denied, or fighting their insurance to pre-approve or cover something their doctor ordered. For instance, in 2019, my insurance dropped me without notice, then refused to pay for a $6,000 ER visit (which didn't even include any treatment). Overwhelmed with Andrea's cancer costs, there was no way we could pay my ER bill. So, that bill went to collections, and they'd been calling me ever since trying to get blood from a turnip. Each time, I'd nicely explained the situation to them .... until the month before I left Alaska. On the final call, I was blunt, honest and brutal. When they insisted that I had to pay, I replied "I'm flat broke, I've already filed bankruptcy due to my spouse's terminal cancer, and I'm leaving the country." All of that was true. (A friend had given me $2,000 to ensure I'd make the trip, and I'd asked my boss for a pay advance so I could pay my first month's rent in Canada).

During the 48 years I'd lived in the U.S., I'd only heard rumors about the Canadian healthcare system. Some of my relatives in Alberta had complained of long waits or delayed care. So, I was curious about what my own healthcare experiences would look like in British Columbia. Soon after my arrival, in the fall of 2021, I went to a walk-in urgent care clinic with just my U.S. passport (I hadn't yet received my Canadian Personal Healthcare Number – PHN). The waiting room time was identical to wait times at walk-in clinics I'd experienced in the U.S. In the end, I paid $80 to be seen by a doctor, get a urine test, and receive a prescription. Then, in the Spring of 2022, with my PHN, I went to the ER for a worsening sinus infection because I worried about getting bronchitis again. My wait time in the ER was identical to ER wait times I'd experienced in the U.S. In the end, I paid $0 to be seen by a doctor and receive a prescription – and no bills came in the mail! To me, that was mind-blowing. Both times I paid less than $30 out-of-pocket to fill the prescriptions.

After my first ER visit, on the follow-up appointment with my family doctor, I was asked not only about my physical health, but also about my mental health. I explained that I was still very much grieving the loss of my wife. The doctor immediately put in a referral for grief counseling, and I received a phone call the next day to offer me a variety of options. I ended up choosing both individual counseling (offered for free through one of the local Indigenous organizations) and grief support groups (offered for free through hospice). After about a month, I received another phone call from the primary care agency that had processed the referral for me to receive grief support. They just wanted to know how I was doing. Did I feel supported? Was there more they could do to help? What was good and what was bad? How was I feeling about everything? I literally started crying. They actually cared. They honestly wanted to know if I was receiving the mental health services that I needed. I couldn't believe it. Imagine: a country that cared about the health and well-being of its people! To me, that was mind-blowing.

Then, in the Fall of 2022, I became a caregiver again. Nathan got a triple infection in his foot (pseudomonas, staphylococcus, and candidiasis). Doctors almost had to amputate his foot. For three months solid, he had gone to the hospital DAILY for wound treatment and IV therapy, requiring care from numerous nurses and doctors, including two specialists. Thanks to the Canadian healthcare system, we received no hospital bills. I nearly had a panic attack when I thought about what that would have cost in the U.S. Again, that experience confirmed one of the reasons I'd left.

As I continued attending grief support groups, I learned that Canadians were astonished and repulsed when I explained our experiences with the U.S. healthcare system, how I was forced to file bankruptcy because my spouse had terminal cancer, how I had to be *very careful* NOT to earn an extra $5 for fear of losing my insurance (Medicaid), how insurance forced me to do 6 weeks of PAINFUL physical therapy before they'd pay for an MRI where we found out I had a torn labrum that the PT had actually made worse, how I'd watched my spouse suffer because terminal patients in Alaska were not given the choice/option of Death With Dignity, how my insurance dropped me without notice and refused to cover a $6,000 ER visit, etc. But in all honesty, our story wasn't unique. EVERY AMERICAN HAD THESE KIND OF STORIES. On the other hand, the Canadians I spoke with didn't know what it was like to have their healthcare tied to their employment or how much they earned, or having to file bankruptcy because their loved one needed medical care, or being dropped from coverage, or being forced to die a long/painful death because there were no other options. Both countries might be considered "First World Nations," but which was more humane?

In one grief support group session in January 2023, someone mentioned their friend who had been fighting cancer for years and recently chose Medical Assistance in Dying (MAID). The discussion was compassionate and full of respect for the person's decision. It made me grateful to be in a place that respected patient's choices for their own lives and deaths, but also, it made me sad that Andrea didn't get that option. I shared with them one of my favorite memories, from exactly seven years prior, when Andrea put her feet in the ocean for the very first time on our first trip to Kauai (and the reason she requested we scatter her ashes there). In the "Broken Circle" support group, I'd already shared Andrea's

Final Journey using Sine's artwork series, and many of the other participants had heard my stories about our experiences in Alaska. One participant remarked, "I complain about our system, but now I know it could be so much worse." Another participant agreed, adding "I'm glad I'm Canadian."

Also in early 2023, I returned to my family doctor because I was still struggling with underlying symptoms of anxiety, depression, and Complex PTSD. The intensity of the grief had been addressed, especially in the hospice support groups, but all the other baggage from my prior life was impacting my relationship with Nathan and the new life we were trying to build together. For 45 years, since Kindergarten, I had been operating under a lifetime of Complex PTSD – for legitimate reasons. Childhood trauma, cult indoctrination, sexual abuse, rape, domestic violence, gaslighting, suicidal ideation, anxiety and depression had been part of my life for as long as I could remember. But it wasn't until I started participating in grief counseling that I realized the full extent. My counselor encouraged me to speak with my doctor about medication. I was reluctant at first, but I finally made an appointment just to appease my counselor. I explained my history and my doctor sent me home with several worksheets, then we met two weeks later to discuss my scores. This was the first time in my life that a doctor took the time to assess my symptoms and score them to determine the best possible medication. He took one look at my scores and said, "Wow, you have a lot of anxiety." It turned out, all those decades of antidepressants were not appropriate for me. What I REALLY needed was an appropriate anti-anxiety medication! I'd lived with anxiety my entire life and just thought it was normal! I didn't know anything else! At almost 50 years old, I'd finally gotten the right meds (for me).

Within a month, I could tell the difference. After a few months, I was truly amazed. I'd never felt that kind of inner peace, tranquility, and calm. Was THIS what normal people felt like? I was blown away by my newfound composure and horrified by the volatility of my entire life prior to that. I felt like I had to apologize to everyone who'd ever met me. I felt that I needed to explain that I'd been operating from a place of extreme stress, overthinking, compulsiveness, and extremes that I'd been doing my best to manage without proper support. To say that proper medication management was a gamechanger would be an understatement. I was finally in a position to enjoy life and do all the things Andrea wanted for me. That's not to say I'd achieved perfection, but rather, I had capacity that wasn't possible before. I hate that it took 45 years to get there, but I was so incredibly grateful to finally have that perspective. All for $10 per month. To me, that was mind-blowing. And honestly, there's no way this book would've been written without it. With that newfound perspective, I realized that not only had I lived with an untreated anxiety disorder since kindergarten, but I'd also endured it on top of dealing with my spouse dying of cancer. Our experience would be stressful for anybody, but the intensity at which I felt it was truly next level. Then, adding that intensity of my anxiety to the grief after her death was simply unsustainable. Most likely, I wouldn't have lasted long if I'd stayed in Alaska. And I most certainly wouldn't have been able to write Andrea's story without proper medical management. For me, it was truly a gamechanger.

In August 2023, just two weeks after Nathan proposed, we honored what would've been my 3rd wedding anniversary with Andrea. It was a mixed bag of emotions celebrating my new engagement to Nathan while recognizing the anniversary of a COVID/hospice wedding in Alaska. It was bittersweet for both of us knowing we wouldn't have met if it wasn't for Andrea. When I told Lane, his response was: "Andrea must be smiling now." Indeed, I thought Andrea must be quite proud of herself. Not only had she successfully gotten me to Canada and set me up with Nathan, but she had probably saved my life. She'd always insisted that she didn't want me to repeat the same experience if I got cancer someday. And that someday came a lot sooner than we'd ever thought.

In October 2023, shortly before the third anniversary of Andrea's death, I had a routine mammogram. The results were suspicious, so I had another mammogram followed by a biopsy. I received the biopsy results just a few days later. The pathology report stated, "positive for invasive mammary carcinoma." That meant I had breast cancer. Before my doctor told me, he'd already sent referrals to the surgeon and the cancer clinic. Thank goodness I listened to Andrea and moved to Canada! At least I wouldn't have to worry about how to pay for treatment! And thankfully, it was caught early enough that the treatment wouldn't involve chemo. The surgeon said, "This is why we do screenings." I was Stage 1 – low risk, easily treated, high recovery rate – basically the opposite of Andrea's cancer diagnosis. They scheduled me for surgery right away. Compared to Andrea's cancer experience, mine was lightning fast! I had a partial mastectomy and sentinel lymph node biopsy – followed by radiation after healing from surgery. The surgeon doing my mastectomy insisted on doing my colonoscopy first – which a friend said was probably just Andrea's way of looking out for me. All surgery, biopsy testing, radiation, medications, and follow-up appointments with the surgeon and oncologist were covered 100% by the national healthcare system. I hated that I had to deal with cancer again, but THIS time nobody had to file bankruptcy!

I went to my grief support group the day before surgery. After knowing everything Andrea went through in the U.S. system, they told me how glad they were that I was doing my cancer treatment in Canada! One lady said, "After what you've told us about your experience in Alaska, I'm feeling super lucky to be Canadian." Another lady said, "Thank goodness you listened to Andrea and moved here!" I, too, was thankful, and I had the best experience at the hospital. Seriously, the nicest and most professional people, from the nurses to doctors to techs to anesthesiologist. I couldn't believe how great everything was. AND I wouldn't be receiving any scary bills in the mail. To me, that was mind-blowing. My recovery was great, and Nathan made it his life's mission to take good care of me. He made sure I followed my doctor's orders, and he even went out to the store in bad weather just to get the food I was craving – just like I used to do for Andrea.

Since early detection is key, and I was living proof, I used my experience to encourage Andrea's friends and family to get all their cancer screenings done. I loved it when friends posted that they'd completed their colonoscopies and credited Andrea for being their motivation, or that they got their mammograms and credited me for being their motivation. Regardless, some people were getting their cancer screenings and would hopefully avoid being diagnosed too late (like Andrea was) and instead be caught early (like I was).

For Christmas 2023, while I was still recovering from surgery, Nathan gave me such a special gift that totally made me cry. I loved it so much. Nathan said he just wanted to give me something meaningful and heartfelt. We both knew Andrea put us together for many reasons and just wanted us to be happy. So, when Nathan had the idea for the gift, he said he looked on my Facebook to find the perfect picture – and he unknowingly chose MY FAVORITE photo of Andrea and I. But then, he got a phone call from the company he placed the order with. They said it was too difficult to do it with a photo of TWO people, especially with that much detail. Normally, they only got photos of one person or one pet. Nathan asked that they PLEASE try. He explained to the company representative how special this gift would be, about how his fiancée lost her soulmate to cancer, and that he wanted to honor the love they had together. The company rep started crying on the phone and said, "That's one of the sweetest things I've ever heard. THIS is why I do this job. Don't worry, I'm going to PERSONALLY make sure this gets done right AND I'm going to make sure you get it before Christmas." And sure enough, he did! After it arrived, Nathan said he opened the box to inspect everything while I was at my dance class, and he just cried and cried because it was so perfect. After he gave it to me, I cried and cried, too. Then, he sent an email to the company expressing our deep gratitude and how much it meant to both of us.

In February 2024, as I was finishing radiation treatment, I was reminded of how grateful I was that Andrea made me promise to move to Canada and get my cancer screenings. She literally saved my life – and prevented another medical bankruptcy. Having experienced both systems personally, I still stand by what I'd wrote 4 years prior:

> The US healthcare system is so convoluted and difficult to navigate. So many different insurance plans, with no consistency in what's covered and what's not, eligibility requirements, premiums/deductibles/co-pays, denials, appeals, pre-approvals, pre-existing conditions, exemptions, and terminations. It's a hot mess. The whole thing makes it nearly impossible for an elderly or disabled person to navigate, let alone an average citizen. Full disclosure: I'm a relatively privileged, educated white woman. But I've been flabbergasted by the hoops I've had to jump through, the red tape, the bureaucracy that I've been forced to wade through as a caregiver and patient advocate for my terminally ill partner. I could literally write a book. What about the rest of us? What about people of color, less privilege, less education? How are they to navigate this system? No wonder so many people fall through the cracks. No wonder so many just give up and die. Most of us simply don't have the energy it takes to fight the system while sick. This system is oppressive, exclusionary, and contributes to structural violence. The richest country in the world has the highest number of bankruptcies due to medical debt. The system values prof-

its over people. Only the rich, or those who have the best insurance, can access this system. The rest of us are left to piecemeal our needs together by applying to this program or that program, this agency or that agency. It's time to end this mess. We need universal healthcare. We need a simple system that deems you worthy of quality healthcare by virtue of being a human being. Period. No more care based on wealth or association or lack thereof. No more piecemeal. We need to make healthcare a human right in this country. Anything less is inhumane.

Keep in mind, I wrote that BEFORE the pandemic hit and blew up the medical system, and before I witnessed how people die in the U.S. when they have no legal options to end their suffering. Even without pandemics and terminal illnesses, Americans experience the inhumane system on a day-to-day basis. They pay more in healthcare related expenses than any other country but receive less care and have worse outcomes. That was a consequence of changing from a non-profit system to a for-profit system over the past 30 years (the same thing happened with higher education). Considering there are 72 countries with some form of universal healthcare — resulting in around 69% of the world's population having some form of universal coverage — there are other ways that have proven to be better (Brazil is arguably the best model for universal healthcare: Any person in Brazil—from citizens to tourists, refugees, and undocumented immigrants—is eligible to receive free and immediate medical care in whatever form they need, from primary care to surgery to prescription medications, with no previous application or paperwork necessary).

Using myself as an example: Even with 3 degrees, I've never had an employer-provided health insurance plan. Jobs with good benefits, or any benefits, are rare. So, my choices were either to purchase insurance on the marketplace or apply for state Medicaid. Although I attempted to, I'd never been allowed to purchase insurance on the marketplace because my income was too low (even though I was working multiple jobs simultaneously that required a graduate degree). So, I had no choice but to apply for state Medicaid – which requires navigating the difficult and time-consuming qualification process, re-certifying every six months, providing proof of income, and ensuring that income never goes a dollar over the limit. I'd learned the hard way that earning a few extra bucks wasn't worth losing one's insurance. However, in Canada, my healthcare coverage wasn't tied to my job or income at all, so I could take on more work and make more money without risk of losing my insurance. Yes, I paid more in taxes living in Canada than I did in the US. But I was happy to pay it because I'd already avoided medical bankruptcy twice within two years (once for Nathan's foot infection and second for my cancer treatment). Using my experience, I've made the case for universal healthcare being more humane. Next, the final chapter of this book makes the case for universal Medical Aid In Dying (MAID) being more humane.

CHAPTER 11: PLEA FOR COMPASSION

A ndrea and I got engaged in 2014 – although we didn't get married until 6 years later. It was a good thing we waited – because she ended up as a hospice patient after a grueling 3-year battle with cancer. If we'd been married, Andrea would've received less disability benefits (because my income would've counted against her) AND I wouldn't have been allowed to be her PCA/DSP (because spouses cannot be caregivers). Even so, we struggled financially during those cancer years – to the point of being forced into bankruptcy. The U.S. system forced terminal patients into poverty, and most states didn't have any legal options for them to end their suffering. And because we waited to get married until she was literally on her deathbed, I couldn't receive any Social Security spouse's benefits. In my opinion, the entire system was inhumane.

As I mentioned in the previous chapter, 1 in 3 Americans will be diagnosed with cancer in their lifetime. In my opinion, making lucrative profits off sick and dying people in the U.S. healthcare's for-profit system was unethical and inhumane. In my experience, the Canadian non-profit universal healthcare system was more ethical and humane. In this chapter, I make the case that Medical Aid In Dying (MAID) is also more ethical and humane – as it gives terminal patients a choice over their own lives – and offers an acceptable alternative to unnecessary suffering.

Unnecessary suffering is the key factor. Consider the example of a suffering animal, perhaps a dearly loved family pet. If that pet were suffering needlessly from a terminal illness, the acceptable and ethical choice is euthanasia. We generally consider that act to be the most humane thing to do. Indeed, Andrea herself pointed out that a dog would get more respect and dignity than she did. She wondered why it was admirable to put a dog out of its misery, but criminal for a person to choose it for themselves.

Most people are personally aware of the unnecessary suffering that results from denial of life-saving medical care. But few have direct knowledge of the unnecessary suffering that results from the denial of end-of-life medical care. In Andrea's case, only IV-administered pain management was effective – due to cancer commandeering her entire GI tract (making oral and rectal medications ineffective) – but IV hospice care wasn't available at the time. In Andrea's case, only IV-administered Medical Aid In Dying would've worked – which also wasn't available at the time. While some U.S. states have Death With Dignity laws, those options are significantly limited by residency, diagnosis, and method. None offer an IV-administered option. Only the states of Oregon and Vermont allow non-residents to apply. Of course, people in non-legal states are further limited by having the ability physically and financially to travel – which means many patients are effectively denied their right to choose.

These significant barriers are at least partially a result of American culture in which death is a taboo subject – and further influenced by religious institutions that lobby against end-of-life choices. However, death is a part of life. Rather than avoiding the subject and seeing death as a failure of some kind, why not appropriately prepare for the inevitable? Not only have patients been requesting options (as Andrea did), but doctors and nurses want and need options. Healthcare professionals, especially hospice staff, have seen first-hand what happens when their patients don't have options.

In the 2015 PBS Frontline film "Being Mortal," Dr. Atul Gawande showed how doctors — himself included — are often remarkably untrained, ill-suited, and uncomfortable talking about chronic illness and death with their patients. In the film, he explored death, dying, and why even doctors struggle to discuss being mortal with their patients. He laments that there's no natural time to have those discussions – until there's a crisis – which is too late. Both patients and doctors often focus on what more can be done – regardless of what is sacrificed – and either unable or unwilling to accept that some situations are unfixable.

Several agencies and non-profits have been working to change the culture around death and dying. One example is the End Well Project (endwellproject.org), whose message includes: "We can create a world and medical system that supports better deaths. We truly believe this community can shift our culture so that everyone feels supported, informed, and empowered as they face end-of-life experiences, whether for themselves or their loved ones." Another example, Death With Dignity (deathwithdignity.org), perhaps the most well-known movement in the U.S., is especially strong in the state of Oregon. Their message, in part, is as follows:

> Since 1994, Death with Dignity has advocated for the fundamental freedom of choice in end-of-life options for all. Proven safe, effective, and above all, meaningful, the Oregon Death with Dignity Act works exactly as intended and exactly for whom it was intended, without fail. Since 1997, these laws have empowered people with terminal illness to have the control they want during the last days of their lives.
>
> Our goal is to ensure people with terminal illness can decide for themselves what a good death means in accordance with their values and beliefs, and that should include having

an option for death with dignity. We won't stop until that is a reality in every part of the country.

We respect and honor the dignity and worth of all humans.

Through political action and grassroots advocacy, we strive to provide all Americans an option that will allow them to die on their own terms. Death with dignity respects and honors an individual's choices, including how they choose to define a dignified death.

We work to create a future in which all Americans have the freedom to make their own end-of-life decisions.

We believe individuals with terminal illness have a right to die with the same autonomy and agency in which they lived their lives. Our work arises out of deep respect and empathy for this most intimate and personal freedom.

We take a stand for the fundamental human right of individuals with terminal illness to decide how they die.

Powerful individuals and institutions have long opposed our work and continue to use their clout to attempt to turn public opinion against us. Regardless of political risk, we have never wavered in our commitment to advancing policy reform that gives qualified individuals a compassionate end-of-life option and, over time, leads to improvements in end-of-life care for all.

A successful legal argument in Oregon has resulted in a settlement to drop residency requirements for people who want to access Death with Dignity in that state. Ending this requirement breaks one of the greatest barriers to a comfortable death: living in the wrong state. We're calling on every state with a Death with Dignity law to drop the state residency requirement for access. The residency requirement in the first Death with Dignity law was meant to be a safeguard against a flood of people overwhelming the state to use the law. The fact is this never happened in Oregon, contrary to the fears of our opponents. The careful use of Oregon's Death with Dignity law over 25+ years means it's time to remove needless barriers and support people everywhere who are facing a difficult death. **No other healthcare options are limited this way.**

Assisted dying, in some form, is legal in the Netherlands, Belgium, Canada, Colombia, Luxembourg, New Zealand, Switzerland, Spain, Portugal, Germany, Austria, Australia, and in 11 U.S. states (Oregon, Washington, Vermont, Montana, Colorado, California, District of Columbia, Hawaii, New Jersey, Maine, and New Mexico). The list is growing. For instance, the United Kingdom (Scotland, Northern Ireland, England, Wales) just passed legislation at the time of this writing.

However, unfortunately, there is no legislation in Alaska at the time of this writing. Many of Andrea's friends, family, and healthcare providers asked me how they could help get an act passed for Death With Dignity in the state of Alaska in Andrea's name (including some with ambitions to get legislation passed nationwide). Over time, the private Facebook group (that Andrea started as a way to keep her friends/family updated on her battle with cancer) developed into a case for action on Death With Dignity legislation. At the time of this writing, a newly formed group in Alaska was starting a grassroots movement for MAID called End-Of-Life-Options Alaska (eoloptionsalaska.com). Historically, every bill failed that was introduced in Alaska – and it's doubtful that something will be passed at a federal/national level without a majority of states enacting their own laws. However, there are organizations specifically designed for the legal fight, so I invited Andrea's family/friends to join them. One of our friends, Heather, an RN, said, "I pray that Death With Dignity could be nationwide... her story is the exact reason why it should be allowed. I do tell her story, and this is one big reason I do!"

Indeed, this book is the result of Andrea's request that her story be told. Many close to Andrea encouraged me to write it, although it seemed to me yet another depressing tale of the U.S. health-care system that very few would read. However, after I had my own cancer experience in Canada and also learned more about how Death With Dignity (US) differs from Medical Aid In Dying (Canada), I realized that Andrea's story could be used to support more humane and compassionate options for people experiencing unnecessary suffering. Opening this conversation can provide insight into the difficult decisions that patients, families, doctors, and lawmakers struggle to make on this topic.

In 2021, journalist Katie Engelhart explored the complexity of physician-assisted death and the "right to die" movement in her book, *The Inevitable: Logistical and Ethical Challenges.* Engelhart said that many patients in the U.S. seeking death on their own terms are forced to act alone, without telling friends and family, because they fear their loved ones will be prosecuted after the fact, and sometimes patients resort to ordering lethal veterinary drugs from overseas.

"When I started reporting the book, I heard this phrase over and over ... 'I'd rather die like a dog,' " Engelhart said. "A lot of people spoke to me about euthanizing beloved pets in their past. They talked about [euthanizing their pets] as being acts of mercy and acts of love — and all they wanted was the same option for themselves." In countries around the world where aid in dying is legal, people overwhelmingly choose to die by an injection given by a physician. Patients without options are flocking to countries like Switzerland with liberal laws open to nonresidents. "But again," Engelhart said, "I find that people end up traveling to Switzerland and dying before they really want to, because they have to be healthy enough to get on a plane to travel around Zurich or Bern and to complete the process for getting final approval." When traveling isn't possible, whether physically or financially, patients and their families are turning to both formal and informal groups online that refer people to different means of procuring lethal drugs. "Most people who choose to end their lives at a preplanned moment are more concerned with things like dignity ... autonomy," she said, which is contrary to the pain and suffering reasons that most of us assume. In other words, people want choices over their own lives, bodies, and deaths.

In Andrea's case, it was both. Andrea's suffering became unbearable, but she didn't want cancer to take her. So, Andrea took matters into her own hands, on her own terms, humanely. She loved herself like she loved all animals and believed in compassionate and painless death for all. There are worse things than death, and that is suffering. Andrea believed this throughout her life and was committed to not contributing to suffering for both animals and humans. She was an ambassador for compassion, humane treatment, and unconditional love for all sentient beings. But for humans, with our ability to choose, she believed all humans deserved the right to options in their own end-of-life care. When Andrea described what it felt like to be starving to death, our friend Shauna said, "Nobody should have to experience that! We'd never let a pet die that way, so why is it okay for a human? I don't understand why we aren't more compassionate in our society." Our friend Taylor said, "People should have the ability to end their own suffering humanely, before it gets to the point that it's already destroyed them in every way that counts. Here's hoping more of the world figures this shit out. And here's hoping we can get better about having conversations about our wishes concerning end-of-life matters, as a society." In reference to an article about someone who received medical assistance in dying, our friend Janelle said, "We can celebrate every time someone gets the choice Andrea was not legally granted."

As the United States' closest comparable country, and as a geographical extension of Alaska, it makes sense to consider Canada's implementation of Medical Aid In Dying (MAID). Please note that for the purposes of this book, I've chosen to exclusively discuss MAID's "Track 1" – because Track 2 wasn't Andrea's experience, and culturally, the U.S. is not ready to discuss Track 2, let alone implement legislation. In MAID's 5th annual report, Mark Holland, P.C., M.P., Minister of Health, said, "The Government of Canada is committed to ensuring that Canada's federal legal framework for MAID reflects the needs of Canadians, protects those who may be vulnerable, and supports autonomy and freedom of choice." The report extensively analyzes 2023 data, with key findings as follows:

- In 2023, 4.7% of Canadians who died received MAID.
- Sadly, 15% of people who requested MAID died before receiving MAID. These findings bring into focus how even modest delays can interfere with a person's ability to receive MAID. The median number of days between the MAID request and MAID provision for individuals was 13 days. This suggests that most people under Track 1, where natural death is reasonably foreseeable, received MAID quickly once they were deemed eligible.
- Cancer was the most frequently reported underlying medical condition, cited in 64% of cases, with colorectal being among the most frequently specified types.
- The top 5 reported nature of suffering cited in MAID requests: 1) Loss of ability to engage in meaningful activities (95%), 2) Loss of ability to perform activities of daily living (87%), 3) Loss of dignity (65%), 4) Inadequate pain control (54%), and 5) Loss of independence (53%).
- Unlike the U.S., Canadian MAID was administered by a practitioner in nearly all cases. While self-administration of MAID is permitted in all jurisdictions in Canada (except for

Quebec), very few people have chosen this option since 2016. There are new provisions for practitioners to assist an individual who has chosen self-administration, in the event of complications with self-administration through a written arrangement.

- People who receive MAID do not disproportionately come from lower-income or disadvantaged communities. Findings indicate that MAID recipients live in neighborhoods across the income and marginalization spectrum as well as in urban, rural and remote communities. When comparing residential remoteness of MAID recipients across different jurisdictions to the general population, the differences are not stark, indicating that MAID recipients are not necessarily seeking MAID because of a remote location and a related lack of accessibility to healthcare services. The findings of this analysis align with those of previous annual reports, which have consistently shown that the majority of people needing and wanting access to palliative care and disability supports have received it: 75% of MAID recipients accessed palliative care services; those who required but did not receive palliative care services typically had access to them.

- There were 2,200 unique MAID practitioners in 2023, the majority (94.5%) of whom were physicians, while 5.5% were nurse practitioners. Involvement in MAID can be emotionally challenging, politically contentious, requiring significant time and clinical guidance with specific training. Interest in MAID has been growing as more Canadians become aware of it, fueling concerns across the country that demand for MAID may outstrip the supply of willing and available providers. It is apparent that the increase in unique practitioners has not kept pace with the increase in MAID provisions: in 2019, there were 5,631 MAID provisions and 1,271 unique practitioners who provided MAID; in 2023, there were 15,343 MAID provisions and 2,200 unique MAID practitioners. While the number of MAID provisions in 2023 was nearly three times that of 2019, the number of unique practitioners in 2023 has not quite doubled.

- In 2023, private residences (37.8%) continued to be the primary setting for the administration of MAID, followed by hospitals (32.7%). Only 6% of MAID cases were transferred to another location due to objections of faith-based institutions.

These findings confirmed that Andrea was very typical of MAID recipients: She had the most frequently reported underlying medical condition (cancer), she experienced all of the top reported nature of suffering cited in MAID requests, she needed the provisions for practitioners to assist those who have chosen self-administration in the event of complications, she had received palliative care services, and she chose her private residence as the setting for her death. She was precisely the patient for which MAID was designed.

In summary, MAID provisions are desired by both patients and their providers. And family/friends endorse MAID options in order to support their loved one's choices and to also avoid putting themselves in legal jeopardy for assisting in alternatives. MAID is the most humane and compassionate option. When you have a dog or a cat that is in pain and near the end of life, you have the option of relief for your beloved pet. Some people would like a similar option for ending their own lives in a safe, peaceful, and legal manner. This option also honors the bodily autonomy and rights of the terminally ill, reduces unnecessary suffering, and gives the dying person a choice. Andrea would endorse Dying With Dignity Canada, the national human-rights charity committed to improving quality of dying, protecting end-of-life rights, and helping people across Canada avoid unwanted suffering. Their motto is

"It's your life. It's your choice" – which reminded me of Andrea's favorite song: "It's My Life" by Bon Jovi.

Andrea has an army of friends, family, and hospice staff ready to fight for legislation in Alaska and call it Andrea's Law. At minimum, Alaska needs an Oregon version of Death With Dignity Law. Legal cannabis was Andrea's only pain management during her final month because it was processed through the respiratory system instead of the digestive system (which had been overtaken by cancer). Therefore, Alaska also needs IV-administered pain management in the home setting for all hospice patients. In a perfect world, we'd have both universal legal cannabis and universal legal MAID in the U.S. – just like Canada. But legally, it will require tiny incremental steps to become nationwide. Because enough U.S. states have already legalized cannabis, it's inevitable that it will eventually become federally legal. The same could be true of Death With Dignity. The good news is: there's no need to re-invent the wheel. It already exists. Alaska could simply adopt either Oregon's DWD or Canada's MAID regulations and protocols. Oregon is the most inclusive of the DWD states, but still far more restrictive than MAID. Because Andrea insisted that I move to Canada so that I would at least have the option that she was denied, I argue that Alaska consider adopting the policies of its most immediate neighbor.

MAID eligibility is always assessed on an individual basis and takes all relevant circumstances into account. At minimum, in order to be eligible for MAID, a person must:

1. Request MAID voluntarily (not as a result of external pressure). Multiple safeguards are in place such as requests must be signed by an independent witness, two independent practitioners must confirm all eligibility criteria are met, the person must be informed that they can withdraw their request at any time and by any means, and the person must

confirm consent again immediately before MAID is provided.

2. Be 18 years of age or older.
3. Have capacity to make health care decisions.
4. Provide informed consent.
5. Be eligible for publicly funded healthcare services in Canada.
6. Have expected natural death that is reasonably foreseeable (Track 1).
7. Have a "grievous and irremediable medical condition." This criterion is met only when assessors are of the opinion that:

> a. the person has a serious and incurable illness, disease, or disability (although, having a disability in and of itself does not automatically make one eligible for MAID);
> b. the person is in an advanced state of irreversible decline in capability; and
> c. the illness, disease, or disability or that state of decline causes the person enduring physical or psychological suffering that is intolerable to the person and cannot be relieved under conditions that the person considers acceptable.

Throughout this book, I generally state that Canada uses the term "medical aid in dying" and in the U.S. uses "Death with Dignity." But medical aid in dying (MAID) is now becoming the preferred and far more commonly used term in the U.S. Oregon called their law "Death with Dignity" back when they adopted it more than 20 years ago, but to avoid implying that people who die without MAID do not, or cannot, have a dignified death, that term has fallen out of favor. End-Of-Life-Options Alaska (EOLO-AK) mentioned earlier is also using the newer term MAID. However, EOLO-AK will be advocating strictly for Alaska to pass the U.S. model of

MAID, not the Canadian model. Every year that goes by without MAID being an authorized option in Alaska, many other terminally ill Alaskans go through painful, awful ordeals without the personal freedom, peace of mind, and peaceful deaths that access to MAID could provide to them. Every legislative session without passage of MAID forces more Alaskans to endure the kind of drawn-out suffering that Andrea and her loved ones went through.

My hope is that Andrea's story will motivate and inspire legislators to do the humane and compassionate act of passing laws to prevent future Alaskans from suffering the same way that she did. Putting the choice in the hands of the patients themselves and their medical providers is the most ethical way to ensure people aren't forced into unnecessary suffering or resort to unregulated lethal alternatives. With already proven policies just over the border, providing this option for end-of-life care ensures that everyone has the ability to choose when the inevitable happens.

APPENDIX A: ADVICE & THINGS
I WISH I'D KNOWN

First of all, cancer isn't fair. Nothing about cancer feels okay. It might take years to wrap your brain around what a diagnosis really means. It is almost impossible to imagine what is happening, especially while it is happening. None of it makes sense. It's unjust and unbelievable. Second, you have every reason to feel what you feel. Anger, sadness, and disbelief are common and understandable emotions. When you're dealing with a diagnosis, it's entirely valid to feel whatever you're feeling. Seek out a grief counselor, or any counseling, that will give you the opportunity to express these feelings.

Unfortunately, a lot of what a patient will experience (and their family/friends as a result) will be dictated by insurance. Based on what the insurance and oncologist are authorized to provide, you may or may not be told about treatment options, what to expect, or alternatives. In my experience, most doctors either can't or won't be entirely honest with you. If they were 100% honest about everything, fewer people would choose to do chemotherapy and that would severely jeopardize their profits. You'll need to be very adamant about getting as much information out of the doctors as possible. Demand links to studies proving anything they say, especially regarding prognosis and survival rates for the patient's specific cell type. Don't allow doctors to lump all cancers into one statistic. Ask about the patient's specific cell type and Stage number.

Cancer and cancer treatments are painful. If you live in a legal state for cannabis, start researching Rick Simpson Oil (RSO) or Full Extract Cannabis Oil (FECO). The only way Andrea avoided opiates and narcotics was by using cannabis oil that we made ourselves in

Alaska. However, if you're not in a legal state for cannabis, the patient will have little choice but to take the painkillers prescribed, which will likely produce a candidate for dependency and addiction. So, if the patient survives, keep in mind that they might be facing another challenge coming off those drugs.

As for the emotional day-to-day toll this journey will take, keep in mind that EVERYTHING will be turned upside down. There won't be anything unaffected. It's not an exaggeration to say that a cancer diagnosis and subsequent treatment will alter every part of the patient's life and body. As a result, all abilities will be dictated by the treatment cycles. Life will be lived based on the patient's ability to function day-to-day, sometimes hour-to-hour. Side effects will entirely depend on which drugs the patient is given. Make sure to read the paperwork about the side effects for each drug. Those side effects will determine a lot of what the patient can and can't do.

Once the patient has a diagnosis, make sure they immediately apply for Social Security Disability benefits. They are entitled to those benefits by virtue of paying into them during their working life. Because of their diagnosis, they need those benefits because many cancer treatments make it difficult or impossible to work. It takes the Social Security Administration 6 months to decide whether to approve or reject an application, so get the application done online as soon as possible. In 6 months, if approved, the patient will be desperate for that money, especially if they're doing an aggressive chemo regimen.

The cost of cancer treatments varies widely. The patient's cell type and Stage at diagnosis will determine which treatments or drugs will be administered. The cost for those treatments/drugs will depend on the clinic/doctor and what the patient's insurance authorizes. To give you a ballpark, Andrea had a mid-range chemo cost at $45,000/month in Alaska. The exact same treatment was $15,000/month in Seattle. According to her oncologist, her costs were mid-range, meaning average for a cancer patient. If the patient's insurance has a deductible and 20% co-pay like a typical plan, then that's still a big chunk of money – which is why so many people end up filing bankruptcy. Be sure to find out whether the patient qualifies for state Medicaid or federal Medicare; these government options definitely have their limitations, but it might be the only choice for non-wealthy patients. Also, most states/cities have a cancer association that helps needy patients with basic living expenses like utility bills and food. With a significant diagnosis, your best bet is to ensure the patient applies for SSDI, continue raising funds on GoFundMe, and prepare for possible bankruptcy.

Most likely, your area has an agency that provides services for disabled people. See if you or a family member can become a caregiver for your loved one. You'll be taking care of the patient anyway, so you might as well get paid for it. The process takes up to six months to get everything set up, so start it as soon as possible. You'll need to fill out paperwork naming the patient needing services, and if known, name who will be the one providing those services. The person providing services will need to complete CPR certification and training classes at the agency to become what's called a Personal Care Assistant (PCA) or Direct Service Provider (DSP). It doesn't pay a lot, but it's something. And it means you'll be able to care for your loved one better than anyone else, spend time with them, and be their advocate.

Everyone assumes the patient will fight, do all the treatments they're offered, regardless of the physical suffering or financial cost. But that might not be appropriate to assume in every situation. Each person will have their own beliefs about that. In total, Andrea ended up doing 52 chemo cycles over 2.5 years. On her deathbed, she said she wished she hadn't done all the chemo because it meant the last years of her life were miserable. Each patient will need to decide for themself what is "acceptable suffering." It's a battle between quality of life vs. quantity of life.

In case treatments aren't successful, find out what the patient's wishes are regarding death and dying. Do they want to die at home or in a hospital? Are hospice services available in your area? Do they want to choose how and when? Andrea made it clear that she wanted to choose for herself when her fight would end. Unfortunately, Alaska had no legal option for medical aid in dying. So, she didn't get the choice she wanted regarding when or how she died. If you live in a state that has Death With Dignity, start looking at the requirements to apply. Many patients who apply don't end up dying with that assistance, but it's there in case they wanted it; the most important thing is having the choice available.

Above all, while the patient's brain is still unaffected by cancer, make sure to draft and notarize legal documents stating EXACTLY what their wishes are. Living Will, Power of Attorney, and Advanced Healthcare Directive are the "must-dos." Once the patient has declared their wishes, make sure you back them up whenever anyone challenges them.

APPENDIX B: REFLECTIONS
FROM ANDREA'S BEST FRIEND

Andrea first began experiencing persistent discomfort in her stomach, which soon escalated into more alarming symptoms. Her abdomen became distended, and she experienced constant, sharp abdominal pain that left her doubled over at times. She struggled with bowel movements, often enduring long stretches of constipation that added to her misery. Despite these clear signs of a serious issue, the doctors she visited dismissed her concerns. "It's probably just IBS," one doctor said after a brief examination. Another attributed it to simple constipation and prescribed a laxative without conducting any diagnostic tests. These appointments followed a familiar pattern: minimal investigation, no imaging or blood work, and an almost automatic assumption that Andrea's symptoms were minor or self-inflicted. Medication was prescribed to manage the symptoms, but no effort was made to uncover the root cause of her pain. Andrea left each appointment feeling unheard and increasingly desperate for answers. During Andrea's initial consultation, the doctor dismissed her concerns, attributing her symptoms to stress. "You're young and healthy," the doctor said, recommending rest and reduced work hours without conducting any substantial tests. Andrea's complaints were minimized, and no further investigation was deemed necessary.

As the weeks passed, Andrea's symptoms worsened. Her follow-up visits brought more questions but no answers. Each appointment seemed to focus on Andrea's lifestyle rather than her symptoms. "Are you eating properly?" one doctor asked. "You need to exercise more," another suggested. The underlying implication was that Andrea's condition was somehow a result of her own choices, despite her increasingly debilitating symptoms.

Melanie, already stretched thin by her demanding jobs, continued to accompany Andrea to her appointments whenever possible. On days when Melanie couldn't be there, I stepped in to help. I drove Andrea to the appointments, sat with her during long waits, and tried to provide support as the medical system failed to offer solutions. Andrea's frustration and exhaustion were palpable during these visits. What infuriated me most was the dismissive and accusatory tones the doctors used with Andrea. Each appointment felt like a battle against a system that refused to take her seriously. I felt a deep, simmering rage as I watched Andrea struggle to explain her pain, only to be met with skepticism and blame. The lack of compassion and the thinly veiled insinuations that Andrea's condition was her fault were unbearable. It was dehumanizing, and it left me angry at a system that seemed designed to fail those who needed it most.

Adding to the challenges, Andrea had recently lost a well-paying job that had provided some stability for their household. The physical toll of her worsening condition made it impossible to keep up with the demands of her position. Losing her job was a devastating blow—financially and emotionally. Andrea confided in me about her feelings of guilt and inadequacy. "I'm supposed to be contributing," she said one evening, her voice heavy with emotion. "Melanie's working herself into the ground, and now I'm just a burden." Her words were gut-wrenching, a reflection of the societal pressure to equate self-worth with productivity, even in the face of serious illness. Navigating the labyrinth of Medicaid and other low-income assistance programs became another exhausting obstacle for Andrea. She spent hours on the phone, often being transferred between departments or placed on hold, only to be met with conflicting information or additional requirements. The application processes were overwhelming, and the delays in obtaining coverage created yet another barrier to her diagnosis and treatment. Every step of the way seemed designed to test her patience and resolve, adding unnecessary stress to an already dire situation. The sheer bureaucracy of accessing basic healthcare felt like an additional illness, one that drained her energy and spirit.

Months later, Andrea was finally diagnosed with cancer. The disease had advanced significantly, underscoring the consequences of delayed diagnosis and dismissive treatment. The weight of the diagnosis hit Melanie and Andrea hard, compounded by the knowledge that earlier intervention might have made a difference. As Andrea's condition worsened, the shortcomings of the healthcare system became even more evident. Early dismissals of her symptoms and repeated insinuations about her lifestyle robbed Andrea and Melanie of precious time. The systemic flaws—including biases based on age and lifestyle—had profound consequences for their lives.

Looking back, it is clear that the dismissive attitudes of the medical professionals Andrea encountered delayed her diagnosis and treatment. This experience reflects broader issues within the American healthcare system, where assumptions and systemic biases too often overshadow patient care. Often, healthcare is essentially wealthcare – for those who can afford it – and the system is broken for the rest of us. Andrea's journey through this system serves as a stark reminder of the need for reform, empathy, and a greater commitment to truly listening to patients.

The discussions about death began quietly, almost as an afterthought. Andrea would weave them into conversations, her tone calm but resolute. "If it happens," she said one evening, "I want you to promise me that you'll make sure Melanie doesn't fall apart." Her words hit me like a brick, though I tried not to let it show. "We're not there yet," I replied, hoping to leave her some room for hope. But Andrea's eyes told a different story. She wasn't asking because she had given up—she was asking because she knew.

Grieving someone before they're gone is an uncharted kind of pain. It's like standing in the eye of a hurricane, knowing the devastation is inevitable but powerless to stop it. Andrea and I spoke more about death as her condition worsened. She wanted to make sure everything was in order: her will, her belongings, her final wishes. She insisted on having these conversations in a matter-of-fact tone, but I could see the fear and sorrow underneath. "It's not fair to Melanie," she said during one conversation. "She's given up so much to take care of me. I don't want to leave her with a mess." The selflessness in her words broke me. Andrea was the kind of person who, even in the face of her mortality, thought first of others. I wanted to tell her it wasn't a burden, that Melanie would do anything for her without question. But the lump in my throat made it hard to speak.

Andrea's love for her daughter was a light that never dimmed, even in her darkest moments. She would talk about her with a tenderness that was unmatched, her face lighting up at the mere mention of her name. "She's my everything," Andrea would say, her voice filled with pride and adoration. Every decision she made, every fight she fought against her illness, was driven by the love she had for her daughter. She wanted to see her grow, to be there for her milestones, and to leave behind a legacy of love and resilience. It was clear to anyone who knew Andrea that her daughter wasn't just her child—she was her greatest joy, her reason to keep going, and her most precious treasure. Every decision Andrea made to extend her time on this earth was rooted in her love for her daughter, ensuring she could have as much time with her dad as possible. Andrea's selflessness knew no bounds.

Her decision to try chemotherapy was another topic of long and difficult discussions. We didn't know if it would work. The doctors were honest about the chances of it working but the odds were still not best given her cancer's progression stage, but Andrea wanted to give it a chance. "If there's even a sliver of hope, I have to try," she said. Watching her endure the grueling side effects of chemo was heartbreaking. Her body, already weakened, fought valiantly, but the toll was undeniable. Yet, she never lost her determination to spend her remaining time as meaningfully as possible. In between chemo sessions, Andrea explored countless alternative remedies. She tried diets, supplements, and even the recommendations from well-meaning friends who believed in the latest "miracle cure." I watched her chase these possibilities, knowing deep down that she was grasping at straws. "What if this is the one thing that works?" she'd say, her voice filled with a mix of hope and desperation. I never argued with her. If these attempts gave her a sense of control or comfort, that was enough for me.

But as much as Andrea fought, I believe she knew from the beginning that this was a battle she wouldn't win. In our deepest conversations, she would let the facade drop. "I'm not scared of dying," she told me once, swirling her glass of the sweet wine she loved so much. "I'm scared of leaving everyone behind. I'm scared of how it'll hurt Melanie, my daughter, you, and so many others. I'm scared of being forgotten." We spent hours talking about her fears. She worried about the practical things—finances, unfinished business—but also about the intangible. I reassured her that she had left an indelible mark on all of us. "Andrea, you're unforgettable," I said. "Every laugh, every hug, every story you've shared is part of us now. We'll carry you with us forever."

Despite the gravity of these conversations, Andrea always found a way to create moments of joy, and music was often her refuge. She loved music with a passion that was infectious. Our special times together often involved blasting her favorite tunes, filling the room with sound and energy that could chase away even the darkest thoughts. We'd pour glasses of her favorite sweet wine, turn the volume up, and let the melodies transport us. Andrea would sing along, her voice soft but determined, a faint smile lighting up her face. These moments weren't just about music; they were about escaping the weight of her illness, even if only for a little while. Music became our sanctuary, a shared world where the fear and sadness couldn't touch us. Those were the times I held onto most tightly—the ones where she was still Andrea, vibrant and full of life, even as her body betrayed her.

Andrea spoke often about her desire to go to Seattle, where the Death with Dignity law would allow her to make the choice to end her life on her own terms. It was important to her to have control over how and when her life would end, rather than allowing cancer to dictate that decision. "I don't want to be at the mercy of this disease," she said. "I want it to be my choice." The pandemic, however, made that dream impossible. The travel restrictions, the risks, and the uncertainty of the world at that time created insurmountable barriers. It broke her heart to let go of that plan; but Andrea, ever pragmatic, shifted her focus. If she couldn't get to Seattle, she would still choose her moment. "I need to go when I still have something left to give," she told me. "I don't want everyone's last memories of me to be of someone who is already gone in every way except physically." Her resolve was both heartbreaking and deeply inspiring. Andrea's strength shone even in her most vulnerable moments, and her decision to reclaim that control was an act of profound courage.

I remember one conversation that became unexpectedly heated. Andrea had caught me talking about her in the past tense. She confronted me, her voice sharper than usual. "I'm still here," she said. "Why are you talking about me like I'm already gone?" I was taken aback, not realizing what I had done. I tried to explain, stumbling over my words, but the truth was hard to admit. Maybe I had already begun to come to terms with losing her, while she was still holding onto hope. That moment stayed with me, a painful reminder of how grief can creep in even before loss, and how it can shift the dynamics of a relationship in ways neither person expects.

As the pandemic forced us apart, these moments became even more precious. Andrea's decision to isolate from me and my children was a painful but selfless choice. She wanted to protect them, her chosen family of nephews, from the risk of exposure. Phone calls became our lifeline, but they couldn't replace the warmth of her presence. I missed her deeply; I just wanted to hug her, kiss her, and desperately wanted life to return to "the before times." The separation took its toll on both of us. Andrea became more introspective, and our conversations about death grew more frequent. "I'm scared," she admitted one evening. It was the first time she had said it aloud. "Not of dying, exactly. But of leaving everyone behind. Of not being here for them." I didn't know what to say, so I just listened. Sometimes that was all I could offer—a safe space for her to voice her fears. I remember telling her, "You'll always be here; you've left so much of yourself in all of us. In Melanie, in your daughter, in the kids, in me. That doesn't go away."

And then there was the wine. Andrea had a particular fondness for a sweet, fruity wine that she jokingly called her "liquid happiness." On good days, we'd pour a glass and sit together, talking about everything and nothing. It was in those moments, with the clink of glasses and the sound of laughter, that the weight of her illness seemed to lift. Those were the times I held onto most tightly—the ones where she was still Andrea, vibrant and full of life, even as her body betrayed her.

The grief of losing Andrea started long before she left this world. It began in the quiet moments, the whispered confessions, the phone calls filled with love and longing. It was a grief that taught me to hold on tighter to the people I love, to cherish the time we have, no matter how fleeting. And even as the pain remains, so does the memory of Andrea's strength, her selflessness, and the profound impact she had on all of us. Andrea's last words to me were simple, yet profoundly weighted: "You've been a good friend. I love you." Those words, spoken with a sincerity that pierced through the haze of her final days, have lingered in my mind, resurfacing in quiet moments of reflection and doubt. They should have been comforting, a balm to the ache of her loss. Instead, they ignited a storm of conflicted emotions that I've struggled to untangle. Had I truly been a good friend to Andrea? It's a question that haunts me. Friendship, I've come to realize, is as much about the love and care we give as it is about the love and care we fail to offer. In the years leading up to her passing, life had grown increasingly complicated, and the pandemic cast a long shadow over our ability to connect. Isolation became the default state, and in that isolation, I found myself retreating, not out of a lack of care, but out of necessity. Still, I wonder: Did my withdrawal leave Andrea feeling abandoned, even as I told myself it was unavoidable?

And then there was Melanie. She was the one who bore the brunt of Andrea's care—the day-to-day tasks, the late-night phone calls, the relentless advocacy with doctors and nurses. I watched from the sidelines, sometimes offering support, but never with the intensity or constancy that Melanie gave so selflessly. Was I wrong to lean on the excuse of the pandemic to justify my lesser involvement? Could I have done more—called more, visited more, fought harder—to be present despite the barriers?

In truth, Andrea's love and gratitude, expressed in those final words, feel like a gift I didn't fully earn. Yet perhaps that's what makes them so powerful. Andrea's capacity for forgiveness, for understanding, for seeing the best in people even when they couldn't see it in themselves, was extraordinary. She wasn't just acknowledging the moments when I succeeded as her friend; she was offering grace for the times I fell short. As I sit with this duality—the comfort of her affirmation and the weight of my guilt—I've come to see that being a "good friend" is less about perfection and more about intention. Friendship isn't a ledger of deeds performed or missed. It's a reflection of love, imperfect but enduring. In Andrea's eyes, I was enough. Maybe that's what matters most.

Still, I can't help but think about what I've learned from this experience. Andrea's words have pushed me to examine not just my relationship with her, but with others in my life. Am I showing up for the people I care about? Am I letting them know they matter to me? These questions linger, urging me to be more intentional, more present, more vulnerable. Because if I've learned anything, it's that love isn't about being flawless. It's about being there, even when it's hard, even when it feels like you're not doing enough.

Through the love, support, and friendship she provided to me, I grew as a person. I learned new skills I was once afraid to tackle, and she taught me the true meaning of unconditional love. Andrea showed me that I could become anyone I wanted to be, and with the skills she imparted to me, I will continue working on a Death With Dignity law in Alaska in her honor. One day, I hope that people facing her fate will have the ability to die on their own terms, humanely and with dignity. Andrea's legacy, for me, is a call to be better, to be happy in life—not perfect, but better. And in that striving, I hope to honor the gift of her friendship and the profound love she carried for those around her.

RECOMMENDED READING

1. *A Good Death: Making the Most of Our Final Choices* - by Sandra Martin
2. *With the End in Mind: Dying, Death, and Wisdom in an Age of Denial* - by Kathryn Mannix
3. *Nothing to Fear: Demystifying Death to Live More Fully* - by Julie McFadden, RN
4. *This Is Assisted Dying: A Doctor's Story of Empowering Patients at the End of Life* - by Dr. Stefanie Green
5. *Medical Aid in Dying: A Guide for Patients and Their Supporters* - by Lonny Shavelson, MD
6. *In Passing: Stories of Medical Aid in Dying* - by Twana Sparks, MD
7. *The Many Faces of MAID* - by Carol Cram & Cynthia Clark
8. *Medical Assistance in Dying (MAID) in Canada: Key Multidisciplinary Perspectives* - by Jaro Kotalik and David W. Shannon, Editors
9. The World Federation of Right to Die Societies – Ensuring Choices for a Dignified Death (wfrtds.org)
10. Medical Assistance in Dying: Overview - Canada (canada.ca/en/health-canada/services/health-servi ces-benefits/medical-assistance-dying)

AFTERWORD

While I really appreciated the care hospice provided, unfortunately, those services are limited in many parts of the world. Andrea happened to die of cancer in Alaska during covid. At that time, the only option available to us was in-home hospice care. However, we learned the hard way that some types of cancer can completely take over the GI tract, from mouth to anus, which renders all oral and rectal medication useless because they cannot be absorbed. Intravenous pain management is the only thing that works in that scenario, which is generally not allowed in the home setting. Without an in-patient option to administer IV medication, dying people like Andrea are forced to endure inhumane suffering while their families watch. In Andrea's case, our state also lacked a legal Death With Dignity option for terminal patients to choose an end to their suffering. This puts both the dying person and their family in an impossible position. It also puts hospice staff in an impossible position because they are not legally allowed to facilitate death, even if it's desperately needed and wanted. As Andrea pointed out, we treat our pets with more respect than we treat ourselves. We'd never allow our pet to suffer the way we force humans to suffer. Rather, we do the humane thing to end suffering. Why can't we choose that for ourselves, too? In Andrea's case, that was an illegal choice. The horror of that experience changed me profoundly, to the point that I left the U.S. I'm now in Canada with the right to universal MAID (medical aid in dying). In the event that I'm ever in those shoes, I want that option available (whether I choose it or not). I do NOT want to be forced to repeat Andrea's experience. Canada has had legal MAID for ten years. Despite the naysayer's concerns, it hasn't led to high rates. Only 4% of Canadians die that way. While I'm a big believer in the value of hospice care, I also believe dying people deserve the right to make choices over their own life and death. Yes, everyone deserves a good death. Using my personal experiences with Andrea, in both the U.S. and Canadian healthcare systems, I hope this book serves to help prevent others from repeating the same horrible experiences. We can do better.

Melanie M. Lindholm is known in Alaska as a graduate student turned adjunct professor and an ex-Mormon turned belly dancer. Her first publication in 2007 titled "Why I Left" outlines her reasons for leaving the LDS faith and coincidentally became her writing sample for applying to graduate school in Arctic and Northern Studies at the University of Alaska Fairbanks in 2012. Her 2014 master's thesis "Alaska Native Perceptions of Food, Health, and Community Well-Being: Challenging Nutritional Colonialism" became the basis for her third publication, a chapter of the same title for the 2019 anthology "Indigenous Food Sovereignty in the United States: Restoring Cultural Knowledge Protecting Environments and Regaining Health." After her life was upended by the cancer and death of her soulmate, Melanie left academia and started a new life in Canada.

To contact the author, please visit MelanieLindholm.com.

ABOUT THE BOOK COVER ART

"I have chosen a particular moment in Andrea's last days that portrays her resolve, her grief at leaving the planet, and your devotion to each other. I incorporated your hand into her hair as a way to signify your love, sort of the idea that you melded with each other." - Sine Anahita

I requested that our hair blend together – just barely – into a tip at the very bottom – so as to make us into a heart shape.
I feel that our hearts will forever be intertwined throughout space and time.